Origami

ARCTURUS

ARCTURUS

This edition published in 2017 by Arcturus Publishing Limited
26/27 Bickels Yard, 151–153 Bermondsey Street,
London SE1 3HA

ISBN: 978-1-84858-650-5
CH002209NT
Supplier 26, Date 0417, Print Run 6319

Models and photography: Belinda Webster and Michael Wiles
Text: Lisa Miles
Design: Emma Randall
Editors: Anna Brett and Becca Clunes

Printed in China

Contents

Introduction

Origami has been popular in Japan for hundreds of years and is now loved all around the world. You can make great models with just one sheet of paper and this book shows you how!

The paper used in origami is thin but strong, so that it can be folded many times. It is usually white on on one side. Alternatively, you can use ordinary scrap paper but make sure it's not too thick.

Origami models often share the same folds and basic designs, known as "bases". This introduction explains some of the folds and bases that you will need for the projects in this book. When making the models, follow the key below to find out what the lines and arrows mean. And always crease well!

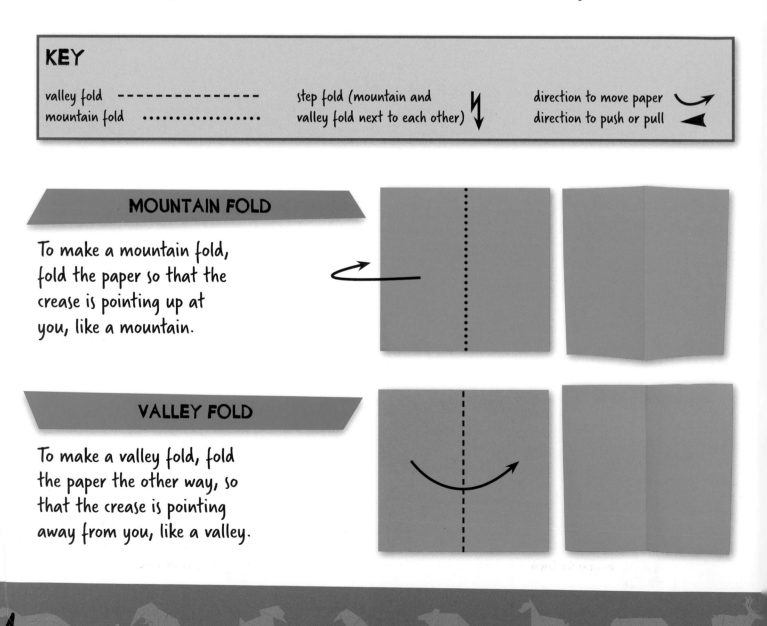

KEY

valley fold ‑ ‑ ‑ ‑ ‑ ‑ ‑ ‑ ‑	step fold (mountain and valley fold next to each other)	direction to move paper
mountain fold • • • • • • • • •		direction to push or pull

MOUNTAIN FOLD

To make a mountain fold, fold the paper so that the crease is pointing up at you, like a mountain.

VALLEY FOLD

To make a valley fold, fold the paper the other way, so that the crease is pointing away from you, like a valley.

INSIDE REVERSE FOLD

An inside reverse fold is useful if you want to make a nose or a tail, or if you want to flatten the shape of another part of your model.

1 First, fold a piece of paper diagonally in half. Make a valley fold on one point and crease.

2 It's important to make sure that the paper is creased well. Run your finger over the crease two or three times.

3 Unfold and open up the corner slightly. Refold the crease nearest to you into a mountain fold.

Open

4 Open up the paper a little more and then tuck the tip of the point inside. Close the paper. This is the view from the underside of the paper.

5 Flatten the paper. You now have an inside reverse fold.

OUTSIDE REVERSE FOLD

An outside reverse fold is useful if you want to make a head, beak, or foot or another part of your model that sticks out.

1 First, fold a piece of paper diagonally in half. Make a valley fold on one point and crease.

2 It's important to make sure that the paper is creased well. Run your finger over the crease two or three times.

3 Unfold and open up the corner slightly. Refold the crease farthest away from you into a mountain fold.

Open

4 Open up the paper a little more and start to turn the corner inside out. Then close the paper when the fold begins to turn.

5 You now have an outside reverse fold. You can either flatten the paper or leave it rounded out.

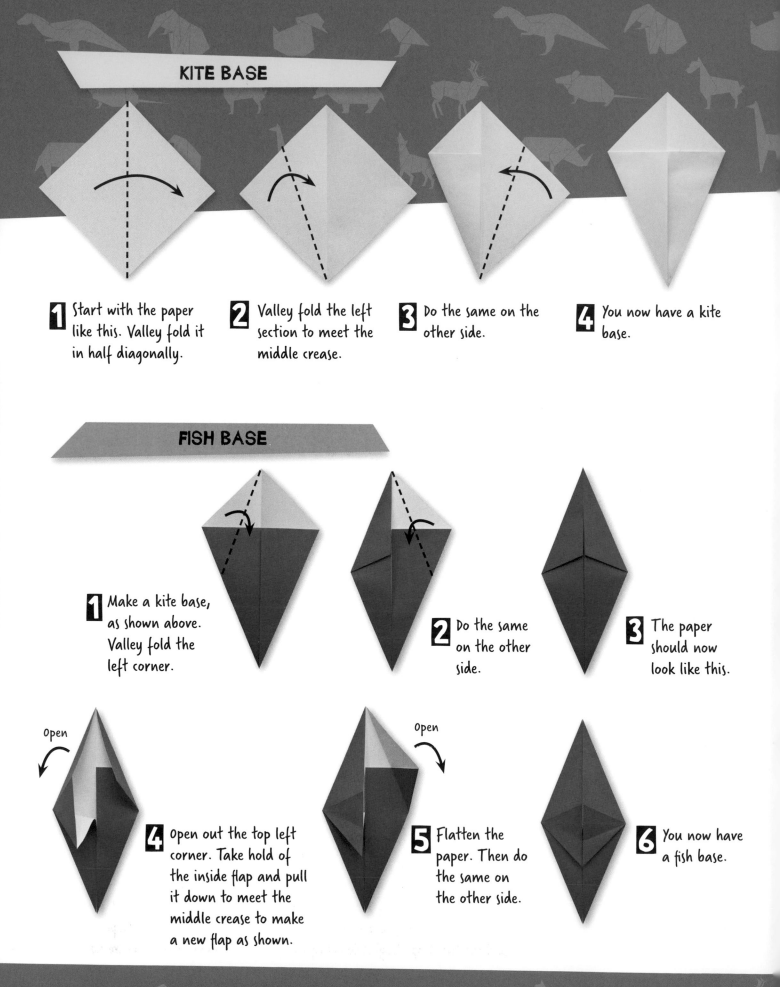

KITE BASE

1 Start with the paper like this. Valley fold it in half diagonally.

2 Valley fold the left section to meet the middle crease.

3 Do the same on the other side.

4 You now have a kite base.

FISH BASE

1 Make a kite base, as shown above. Valley fold the left corner.

2 Do the same on the other side.

3 The paper should now look like this.

Open

4 Open out the top left corner. Take hold of the inside flap and pull it down to meet the middle crease to make a new flap as shown.

Open

5 Flatten the paper. Then do the same on the other side.

6 You now have a fish base.

WATERBOMB BASE

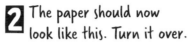

1 Start with a square of paper, like this. Make two diagonal valley folds.

2 The paper should now look like this. Turn it over.

3 Make two valley folds along the horizontal and vertical lines.

Push   Push

4 Push the paper into this shape, so the middle point pops up.

5 Push the sides in, bringing the back and front sections together.

6 Flatten the paper. You now have a waterbomb base.

SQUARE BASE

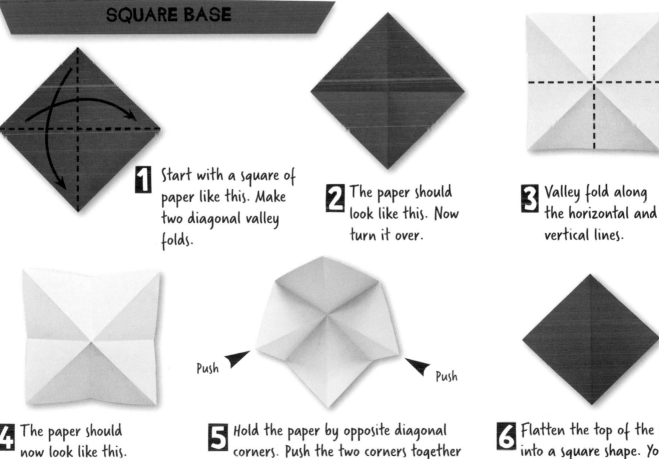

1 Start with a square of paper like this. Make two diagonal valley folds.

2 The paper should look like this. Now turn it over.

3 Valley fold along the horizontal and vertical lines.

4 The paper should now look like this.

Push   Push

5 Hold the paper by opposite diagonal corners. Push the two corners together so that the shape begins to collapse.

6 Flatten the top of the paper into a square shape. You now have a square base.

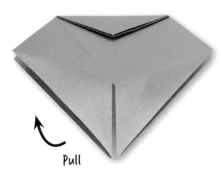

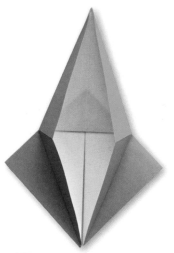

1 Start with a square base, as shown on page 7, with the open end nearest to you. Valley fold the top left flap to the middle crease.

2 Do the same on the other side.

3 Valley fold the top triangle.

Pull

4 Unfold the top and sides and you have the shape shown here.

5 Take the bottom corner and begin to open out the upper flap by gently pulling up.

6 The paper should open like a bird's beak. Open out the flap as far as it will go.

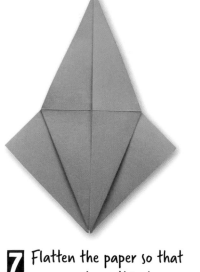

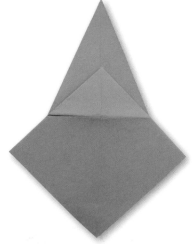

7 Flatten the paper so that you now have this shape. Turn the paper over.

8 The paper should now look like this. Repeat steps 1 to 7 on this side.

9 You now have a bird base. The two flaps at the bottom are separated by an open slit.

Sea creatures

In this chapter, find out how to make a wonderful origami undersea world, from a swiftly swimming dolphin to a dangerous ray with a sting in its tail!

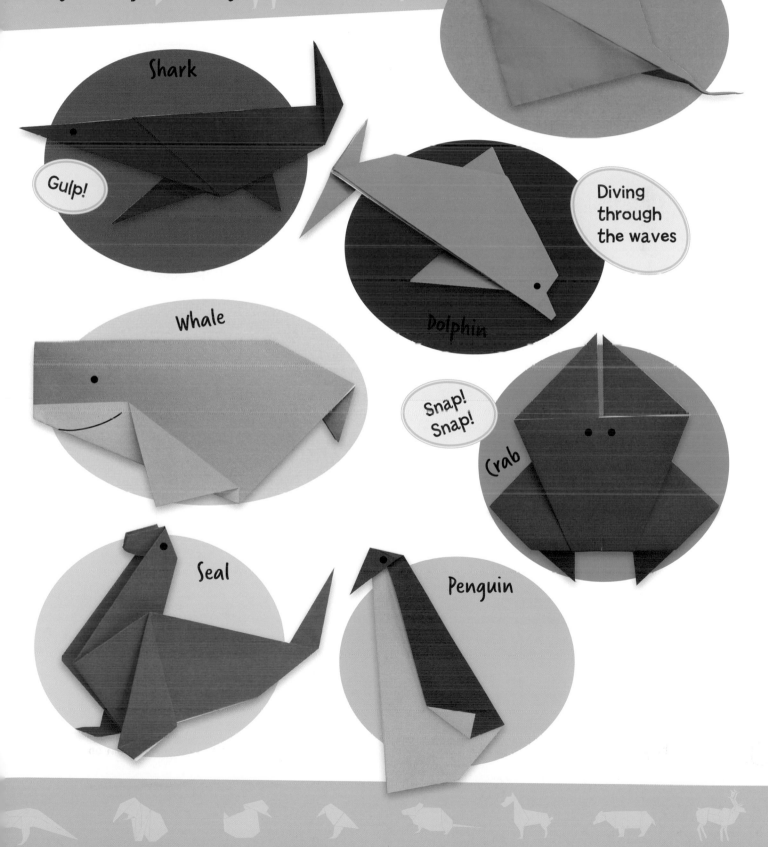

Penguin

The penguin is a brilliant swimmer but it waddles on land. So don't worry if your origami model wobbles — it just makes it more realistic!

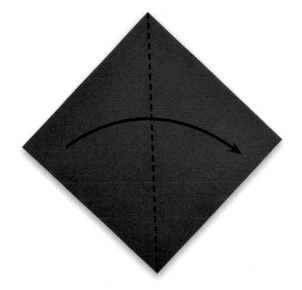

1 Turn the paper so one point is facing down. Valley fold it in half from left to right.

2 Open it out. Turn the paper over so that the crease becomes a mountain fold. Valley fold the right corner.

3 Do the same on the other side.

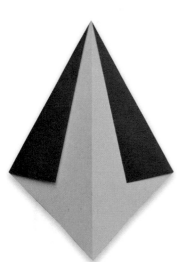

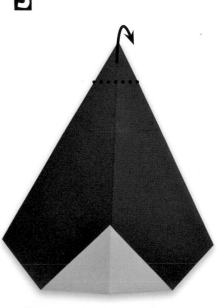

4 The paper should now look like this.

5 Turn the paper over and valley fold the bottom.

6 Mountain fold the top of the paper over.

7 Valley fold the paper in half from left to right.

8 Valley fold the corner tip. This is the penguin's wing. Do the same on the other side.

 Pull

9 Now pull up the beak.

10 Stand up the model and your origami penguin is complete!

Whale

The blue whale is the biggest animal to have ever lived, bigger even than the biggest dinosaur. A real one would be about 200 times longer than your model!

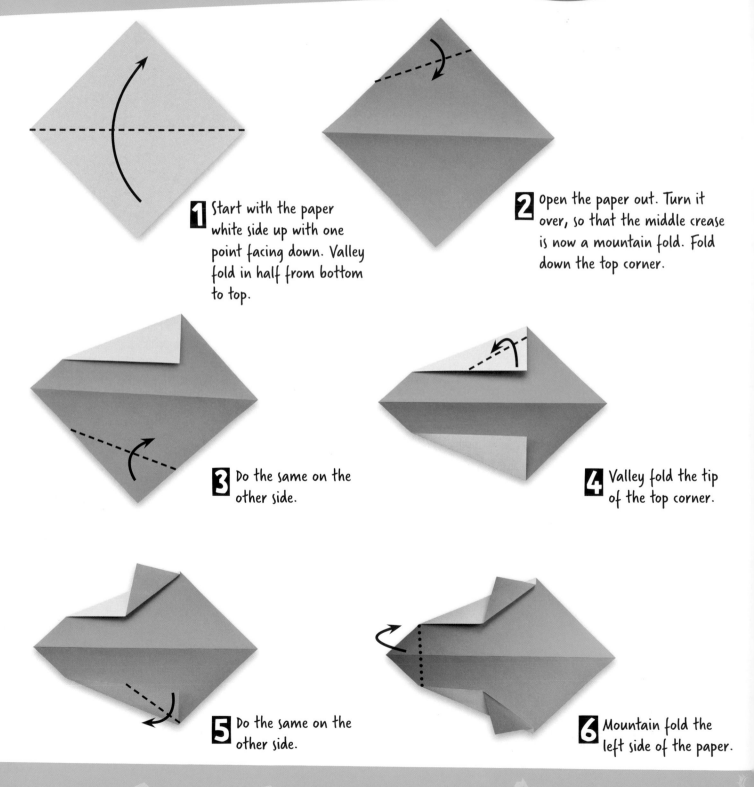

1 Start with the paper white side up with one point facing down. Valley fold in half from bottom to top.

2 Open the paper out. Turn it over, so that the middle crease is now a mountain fold. Fold down the top corner.

3 Do the same on the other side.

4 Valley fold the tip of the top corner.

5 Do the same on the other side.

6 Mountain fold the left side of the paper.

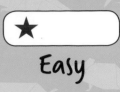
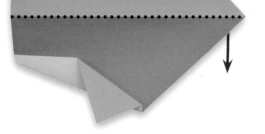

7 Mountain fold the paper in half along the middle crease, so that the top folds under the bottom.

8 Mountain fold the right corner. Unfold, then make an inside reverse fold to create the tail.

9 Now draw on a smiley face and you have an origami whale!

Seal

The seal is clumsy on land and uses its flippers to pull itself along. In the sea, though, it speeds through the water, twisting and turning.

START WITH A FISH BASE

1 Find out how to make a fish base on page 6. With the flaps pointing right, fold it in half so that the bottom goes under the top section.

2 Mountain fold the left point.

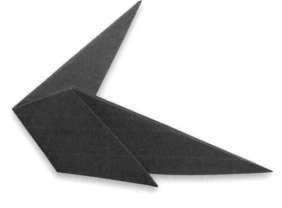

3 Unfold, then make an inside reverse fold to create the seal's neck.

4 Looking from above, you should now be able to see the inside reverse fold, as shown above.

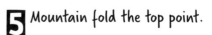

5 Mountain fold the top point.

14

Close-up of head.

6 Unfold, then make an inside reverse fold to create the seal's head.

7 Valley fold the flippers forward on both sides. Mountain fold the tip of the seal's head.

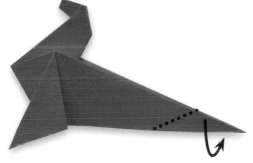

9 Unfold, then make an inside reverse fold to create the tail. On one of the flippers, valley fold the tip of the flap.

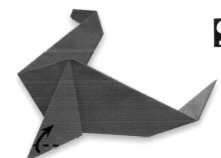

8 Unfold, then tuck in the seal's nose to make it blunt. Mountain fold the right point.

11 Now your origami seal is standing up and ready to clap its flippers!

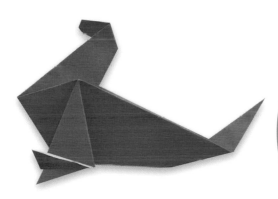

10 Valley fold the tip of the other flipper.

Dolphin

Dolphins are supposed to bring good luck to sailors. Maybe this origami version will do the same for you!

START WITH A WATERBOMB BASE

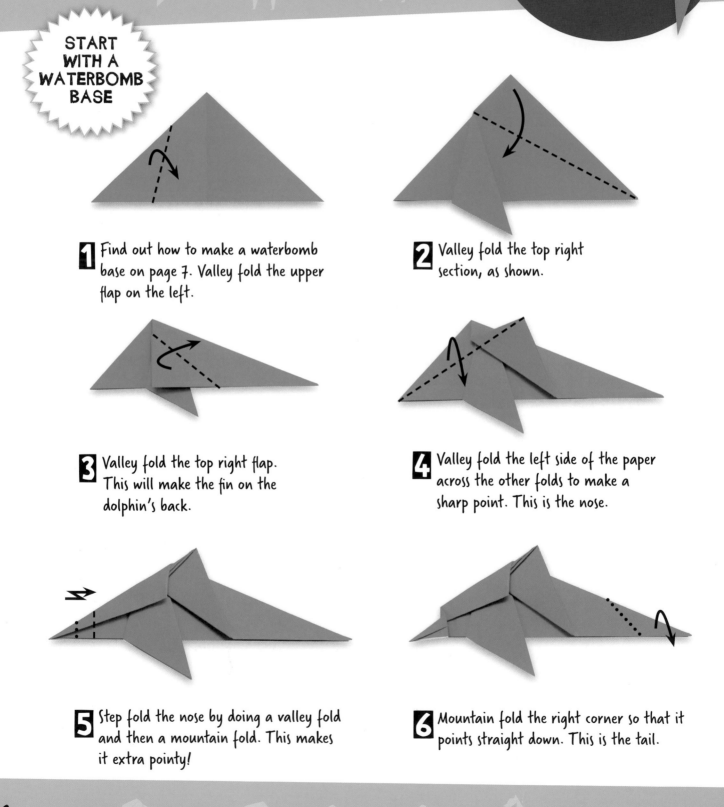

1 Find out how to make a waterbomb base on page 7. Valley fold the upper flap on the left.

2 Valley fold the top right section, as shown.

3 Valley fold the top right flap. This will make the fin on the dolphin's back.

4 Valley fold the left side of the paper across the other folds to make a sharp point. This is the nose.

5 Step fold the nose by doing a valley fold and then a mountain fold. This makes it extra pointy!

6 Mountain fold the right corner so that it points straight down. This is the tail.

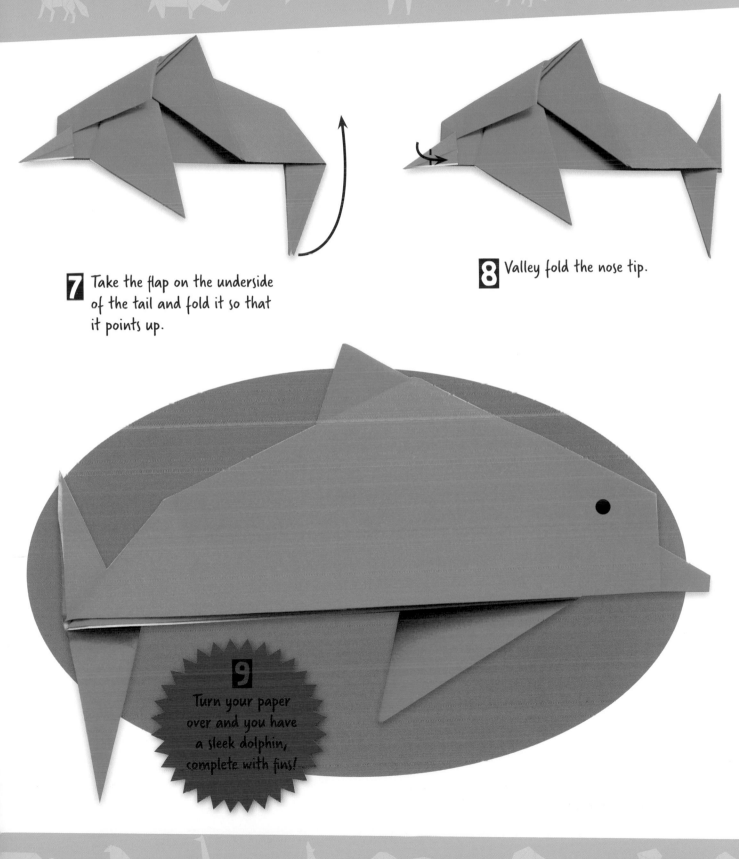

7 Take the flap on the underside of the tail and fold it so that it points up.

8 Valley fold the nose tip.

9 Turn your paper over and you have a sleek dolphin, complete with fins!

Crab

A crab has eight legs, two big claws, and walks sideways!
Check out the claws on this simple origami model version...

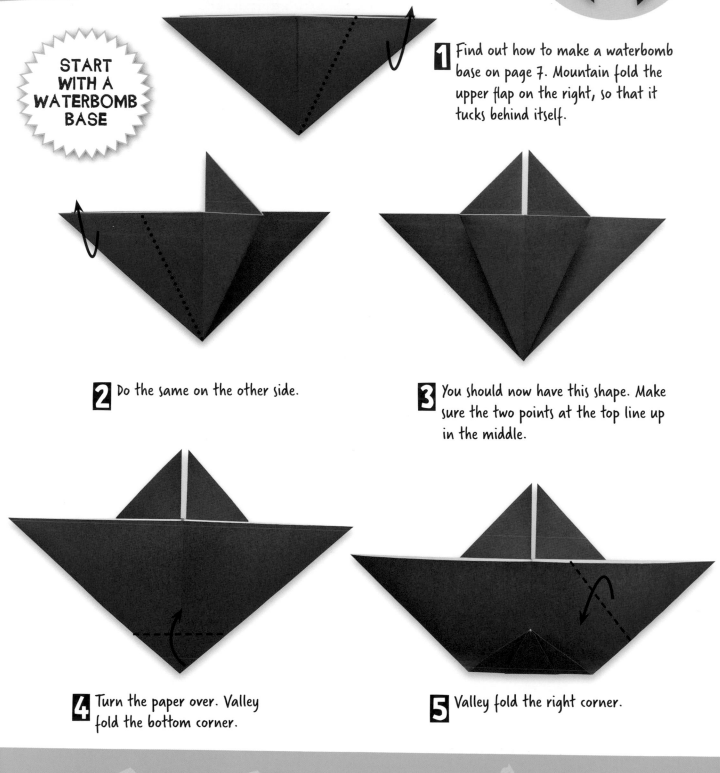

START WITH A WATERBOMB BASE

1 Find out how to make a waterbomb base on page 7. Mountain fold the upper flap on the right, so that it tucks behind itself.

2 Do the same on the other side.

3 You should now have this shape. Make sure the two points at the top line up in the middle.

4 Turn the paper over. Valley fold the bottom corner.

5 Valley fold the right corner.

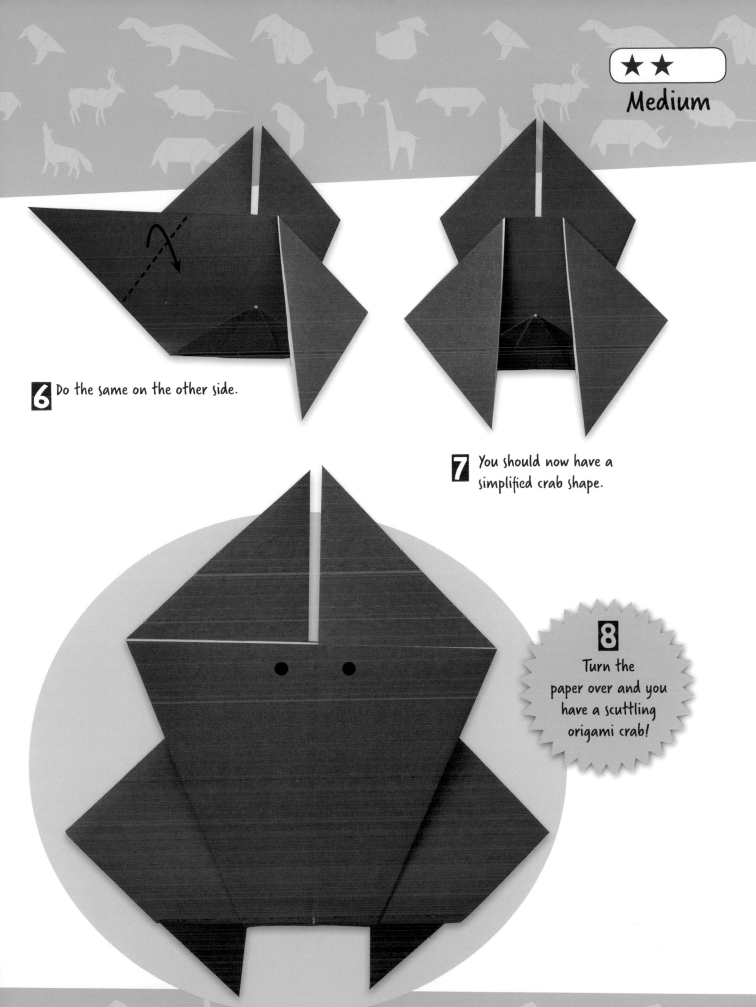

6 Do the same on the other side.

7 You should now have a simplified crab shape.

8 Turn the paper over and you have a scuttling origami crab!

Shark

Sharks glide through the water in search of prey. This dangerous-looking origami shark has its mouth open wide, ready to bite...

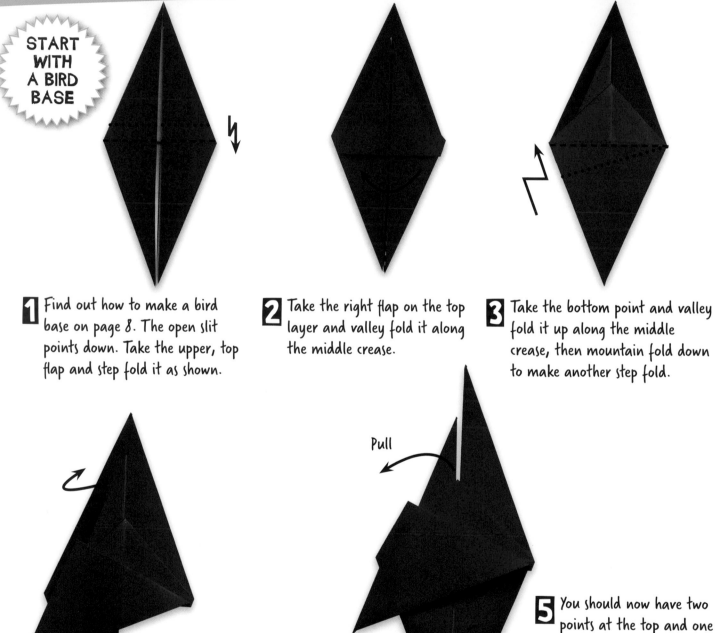

START WITH A BIRD BASE

1 Find out how to make a bird base on page 8. The open slit points down. Take the upper, top flap and step fold it as shown.

2 Take the right flap on the top layer and valley fold it along the middle crease.

3 Take the bottom point and valley fold it up along the middle crease, then mountain fold down to make another step fold.

4 Take the flap on the bottom layer of the left side and swing it back under the right side. Flatten it.

Pull

5 You should now have two points at the top and one point at the bottom. Take the top left point and pull it down into the position shown in step 6.

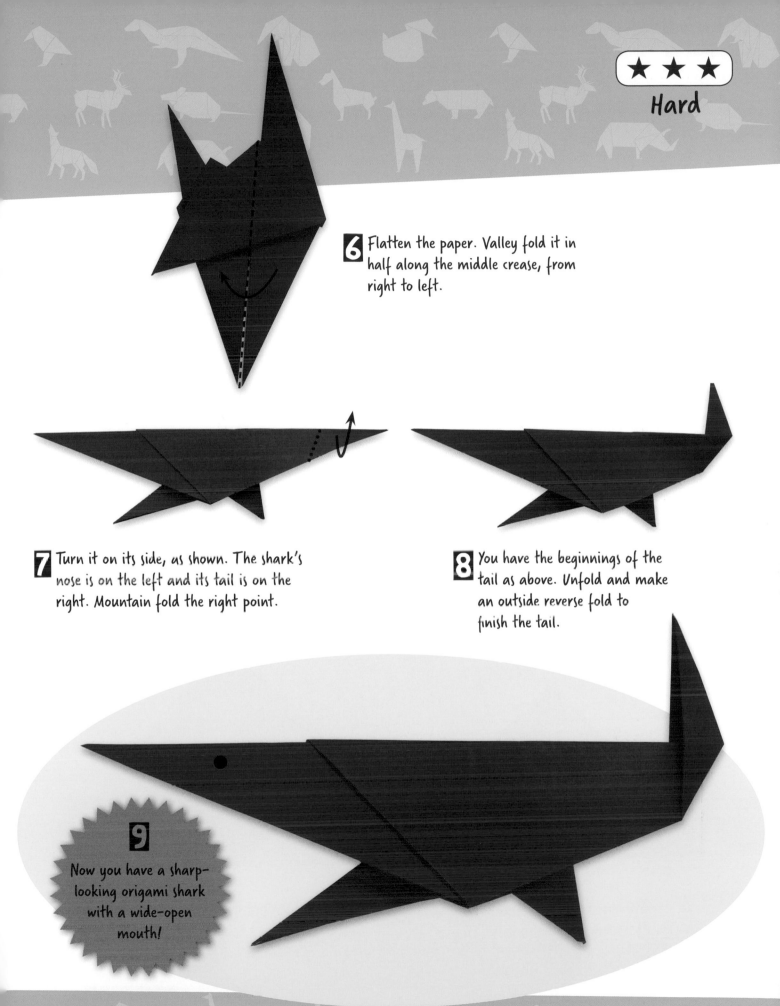

6 Flatten the paper. Valley fold it in half along the middle crease, from right to left.

7 Turn it on its side, as shown. The shark's nose is on the left and its tail is on the right. Mountain fold the right point.

8 You have the beginnings of the tail as above. Unfold and make an outside reverse fold to finish the tail.

9
Now you have a sharp-looking origami shark with a wide-open mouth!

Ray

The ray has a flat body so that it can glide easily through the water. And watch out for that pointy tail, which can give a nasty electric shock!

START WITH A SQUARE BASE

1 Find out how to make a square base on page 7. With the open ends at the top, fold in the upper flap on the top right of the paper.

2 Do the same on the other side.

3 Valley fold the bottom triangle up.

4 Open out the folds that you made in steps 1-3.

5 The paper should now look like this, opened out.

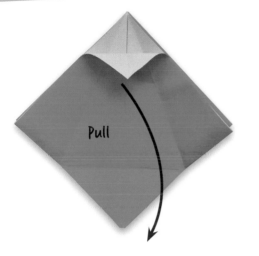

6 Gently pull the upper flap out and down to open up the middle of the paper.

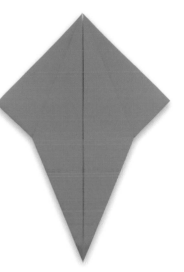

7 Pull it out until it looks like an open bird's beak.

8 Now flatten the paper so that it looks like this.

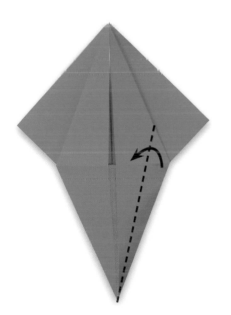

9 Valley fold the right side of the paper to meet the middle crease.

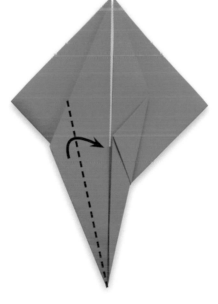

10 Do the same on the other side.

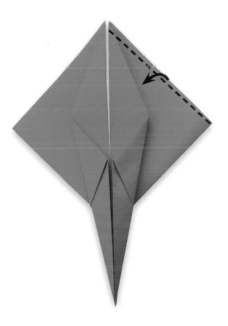

11 Valley fold the right edge of the paper.

Ray... continued

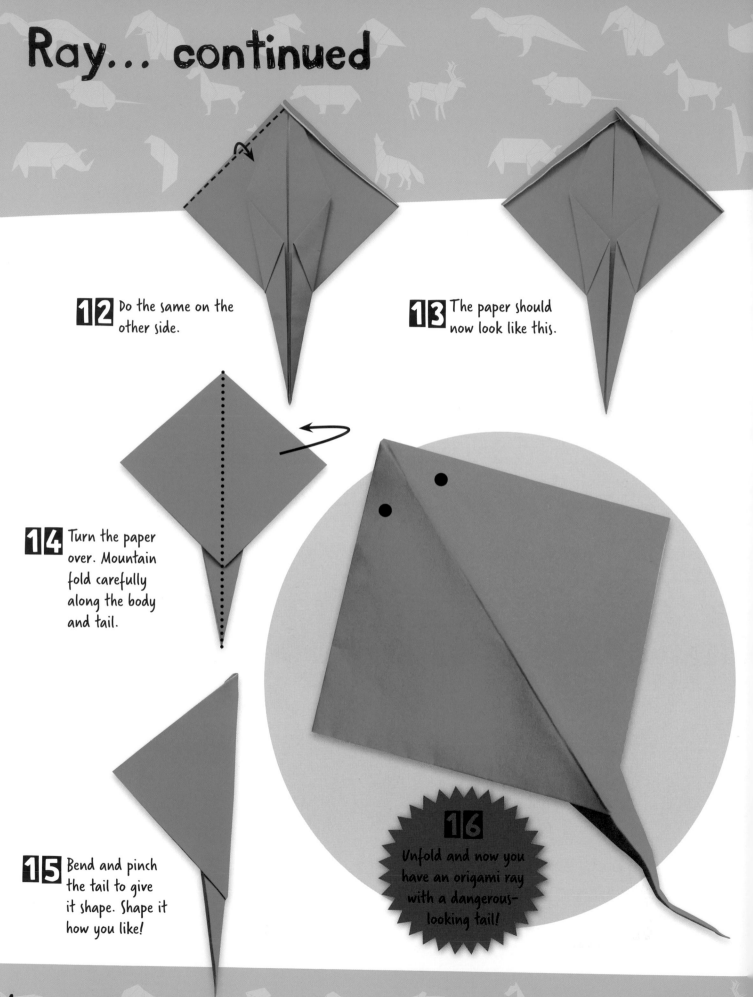

12 Do the same on the other side.

13 The paper should now look like this.

14 Turn the paper over. Mountain fold carefully along the body and tail.

15 Bend and pinch the tail to give it shape. Shape it how you like!

16 Unfold and now you have an origami ray with a dangerous-looking tail!

Farm animals

Create your very own farm! You'll be kept busy making these lovely origami animals — from a cute pig to a rooster with a beautiful tail.

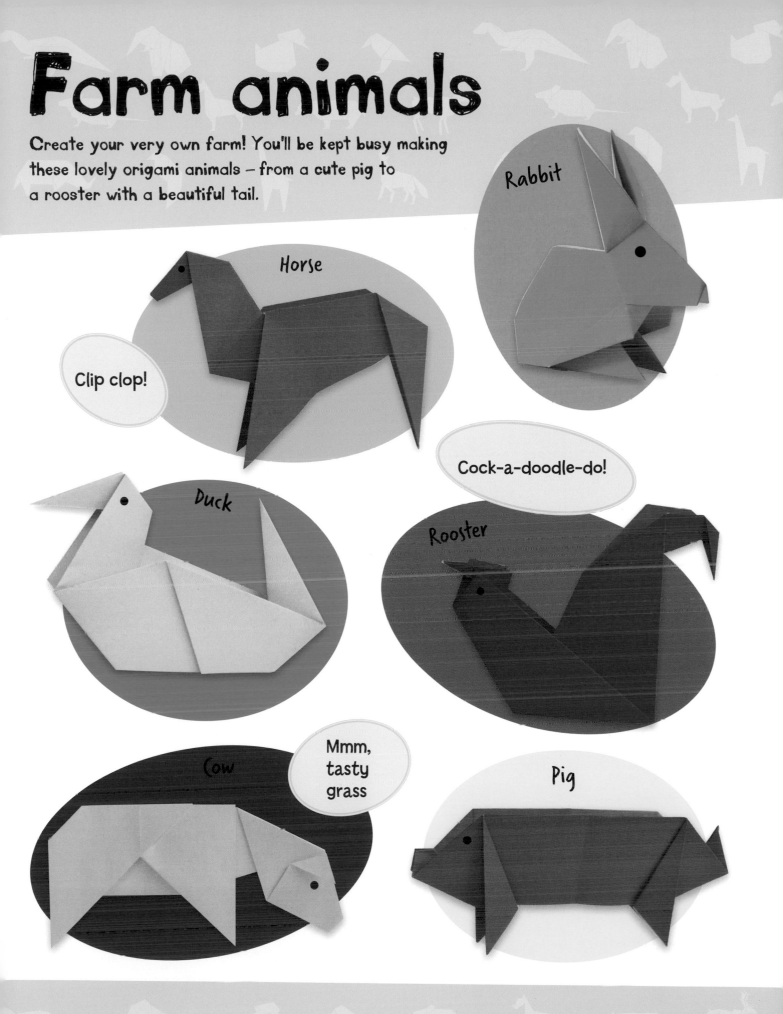

Pig

This cute origami pig stands up on its four pointy feet. A pig's feet are called trotters.

1 Start with a square of paper, white side up. Valley fold the paper in half.

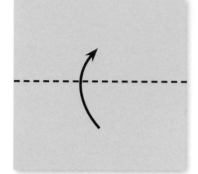

2 Open out the paper. Valley fold the bottom section into the middle crease.

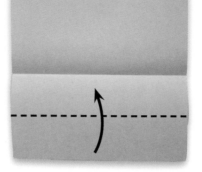

3 Do the same for the top section.

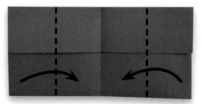

4 Valley fold in half from left to right.

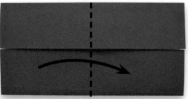

5 The paper should now look like this. Unfold step 4.

6 Valley fold the outer sections to the middle crease.

7 The paper should now look like this. Unfold step 6.

8 Valley fold the top right corner.

9 Do the same for the other corners.

10 The paper should now look like this.

Open up

11 Gently open up the top right corner.

12 Flatten it down into a triangle. Do the same for the other corners.

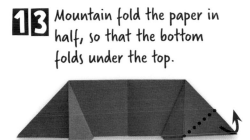

13 Mountain fold the paper in half, so that the bottom folds under the top.

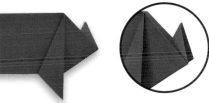

14 Valley fold the right flaps, front and back, to make two back legs.

15 Repeat step 14 to make two front legs.

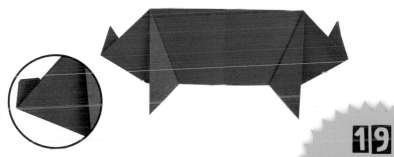

16 Mountain fold the right point.

17 Unfold, then make an inside reverse fold to create the tail. Now mountain fold the left point.

Close-up of tail

18 Unfold, then make an inside reverse fold to create the nose. Tuck the end inside to make it blunt.

Close-up of nose

19 Now stand your origami pig up on its trotters!

27

Duck

The duck spends a lot of time swimming on lakes and ponds. Its feathers are so waterproof that when it dives under water, the top layer of feathers keeps the others dry.

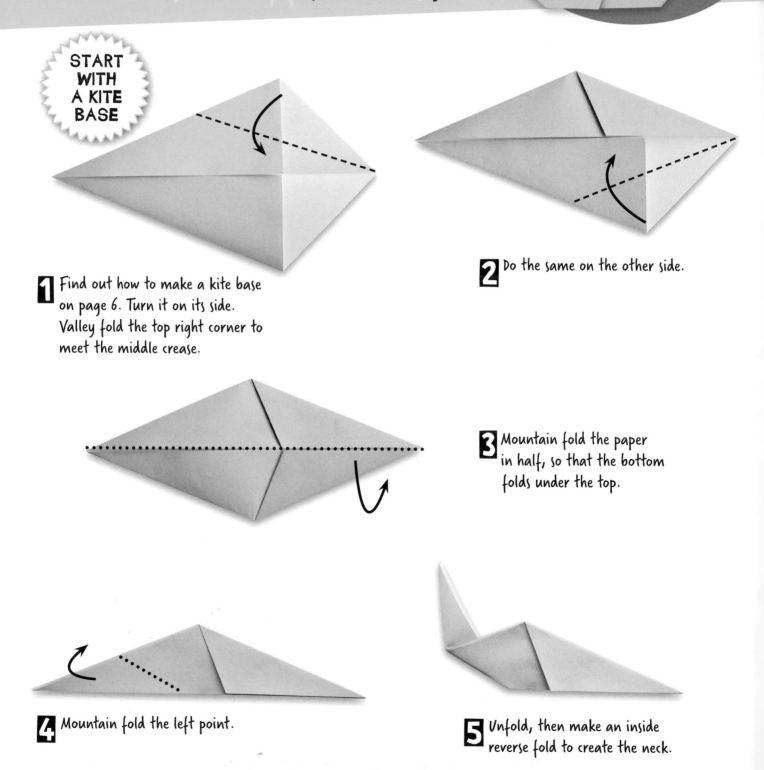

START WITH A KITE BASE

1 Find out how to make a kite base on page 6. Turn it on its side. Valley fold the top right corner to meet the middle crease.

2 Do the same on the other side.

3 Mountain fold the paper in half, so that the bottom folds under the top.

4 Mountain fold the left point.

5 Unfold, then make an inside reverse fold to create the neck.

6 Mountain fold the right point.

7 Unfold, then make an inside reverse fold to create the tail.

8 Mountain fold the left point.

9 Unfold, then make an inside reverse fold to create the head.

10 Balance the model upright and now you have a little origami duck, ready to swim away!

Rooster

A rooster is a male chicken. He has long, impressive tail feathers, which he uses to show off to the females. Check out this origami rooster's tail.

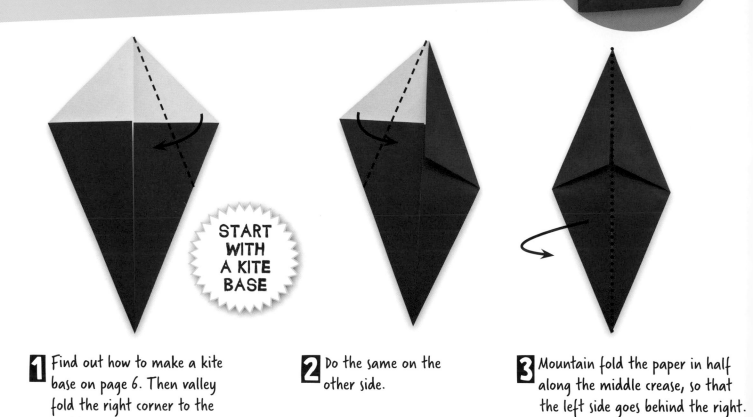

START WITH A KITE BASE

1 Find out how to make a kite base on page 6. Then valley fold the right corner to the middle crease.

2 Do the same on the other side.

3 Mountain fold the paper in half along the middle crease, so that the left side goes behind the right.

Flaps are on the left

4 Turn the paper on its side. Mountain fold the left point.

5 Unfold, then make an outside reverse fold to create the neck.

6 Mountain fold the right point.

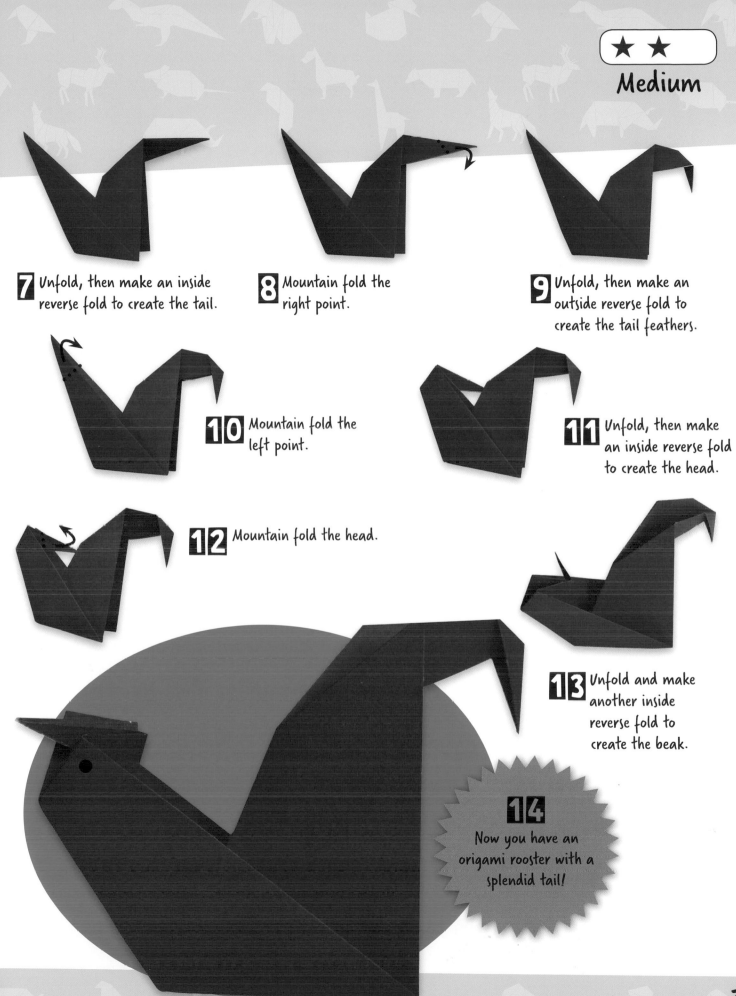

7 Unfold, then make an inside reverse fold to create the tail.

8 Mountain fold the right point.

9 Unfold, then make an outside reverse fold to create the tail feathers.

10 Mountain fold the left point.

11 Unfold, then make an inside reverse fold to create the head.

12 Mountain fold the head.

13 Unfold and make another inside reverse fold to create the beak.

14 Now you have an origami rooster with a splendid tail!

Rabbit

The rabbit has sensitive ears that can be turned in any direction to pick up sounds. Here's how to make an origami version – complete with long ears!

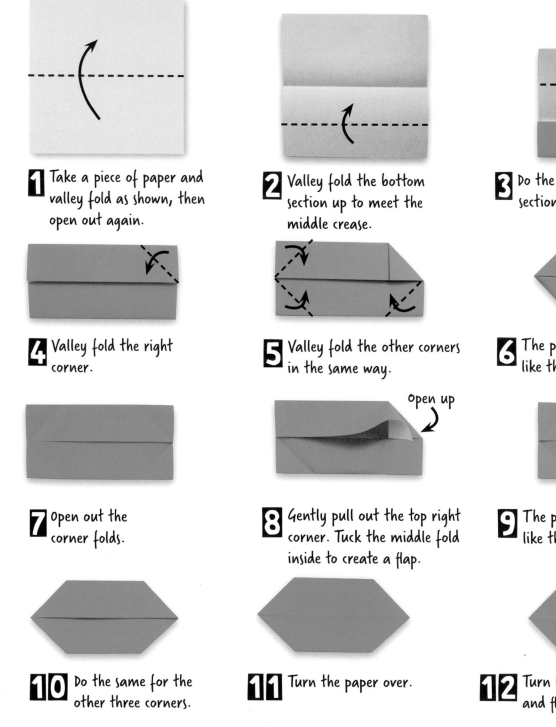

1 Take a piece of paper and valley fold as shown, then open out again.

2 Valley fold the bottom section up to meet the middle crease.

3 Do the same for the top section.

4 Valley fold the right corner.

5 Valley fold the other corners in the same way.

6 The paper should now look like this.

Open up

7 Open out the corner folds.

8 Gently pull out the top right corner. Tuck the middle fold inside to create a flap.

9 The paper should now look like this.

10 Do the same for the other three corners.

11 Turn the paper over.

12 Turn back the right flap and flatten down.

  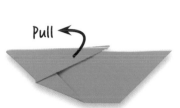

13 Repeat steps 11 and 12 for the left side.

14 Turn the paper over. Valley fold the top left corner.

15 Do the same on the bottom left.

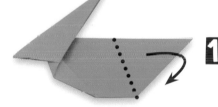

16 Valley fold the left flaps, so that the left point springs into place. These are the rabbit's ears.

17 Mountain fold along the middle crease, so that the top folds behind.

Pull

18 Gently pull the ears up into position.

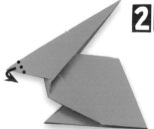

19 Flatten the paper. Mountain fold the right point.

22
Gently puff out the long ears to give them their shape – and you have your origami rabbit!

20 Unfold, then make an inside reverse fold to create the feet. Mountain fold across the nose.

21 Unfold, then tuck in the nose.

Horse

The horse is known for its speed and is one of the fastest animals on land. It has four different types of movement – walking, trotting, cantering, and galloping!

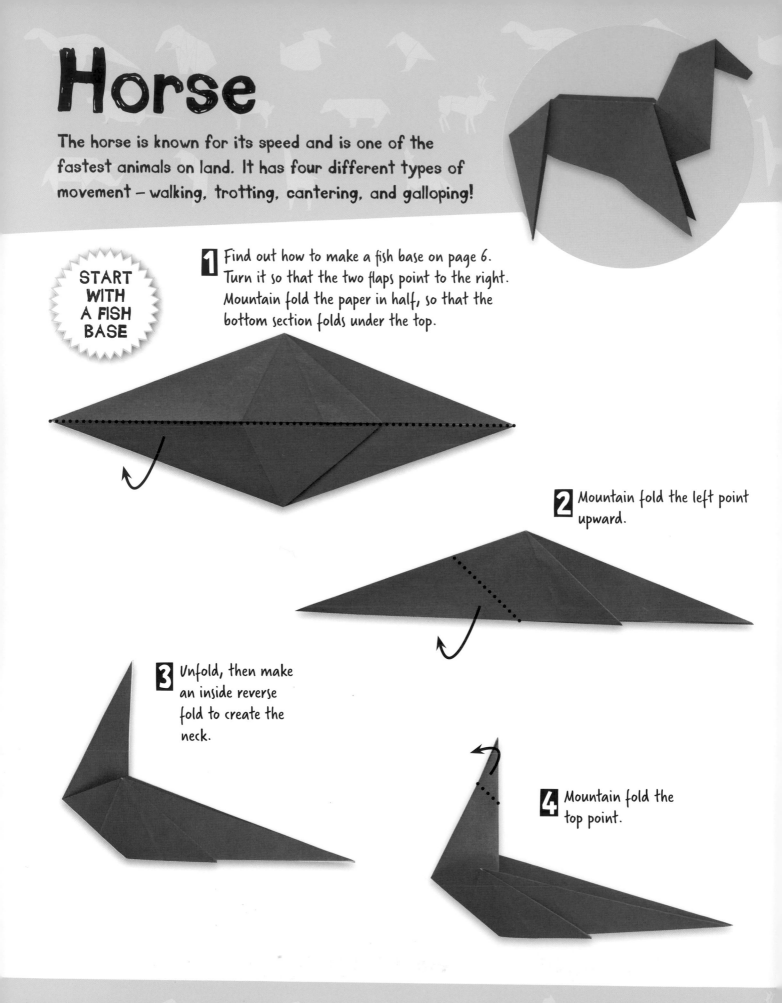

START WITH A FISH BASE

1 Find out how to make a fish base on page 6. Turn it so that the two flaps point to the right. Mountain fold the paper in half, so that the bottom section folds under the top.

2 Mountain fold the left point upward.

3 Unfold, then make an inside reverse fold to create the neck.

4 Mountain fold the top point.

34

Close-up
of head

5 Unfold, then make an inside reverse fold to create the head. Mountain fold the left point.

6 Unfold, then tuck the tip in to make the nose blunt. Valley fold the flaps forward to create the front legs.

7 Mountain fold the right point.

8 Unfold, then make an outside reverse fold to create the back legs.

9 Stand up your origami horse on its strong legs — it's ready to gallop away!

35

Cow

In order to produce all the milk we need, cows need to eat a lot of grass and drink a plenty of water every day.

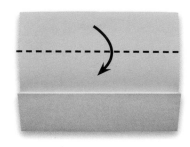

MAKE THE HEAD

1 Start with the paper white side up. Valley fold the paper in half, then open it again.

2 Valley fold the bottom section up to meet the middle crease.

3 Do the same for the top section.

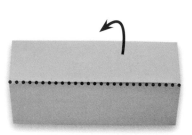

4 Mountain fold the top half back under the bottom half.

5 Valley fold the right corner flap up.

6 Gently open up the top corner.

7 You should see a triangle shape begin to form.

8 Flatten down the paper.

9 Turn the paper over and repeat steps 5 through to 8. From above, the paper looks like this.

10 Turn the paper back over. Mountain fold the right tip.

Close-up of nose

11 Unfold, then tuck the tip back into the crease with an inside reverse fold to create the nose.

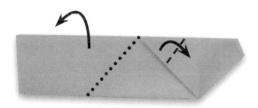

12 Valley fold the right corner of the flap to create ears on both sides. Mountain fold the left side.

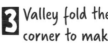

13 Valley fold the bottom corner to make a triangle.

14 The paper should now look like this.

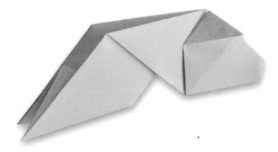

15 Unfold the triangle, then make an inside reverse fold for slotting onto the body.

Cow... continued

MAKE THE BODY

START WITH A WATERBOMB BASE

1 Find out how to make a waterbomb base on page 7. Valley fold the left tip.

open here

2 Gently open the base from the right.

3 Continue opening the base. A triangle shape will appear at the top and bottom. Flatten both sides down, as shown above.

4 Valley fold the paper in half from top to bottom.

5 Turn the paper over. Mountain fold the left corner. Unfold, then make an inside reverse fold to shape the cow's body.

PUT THE COW TOGETHER

1 Slot the head into the body so that it grips firmly.

2 Your origami cow has its head bent down to graze on the tasty grass!

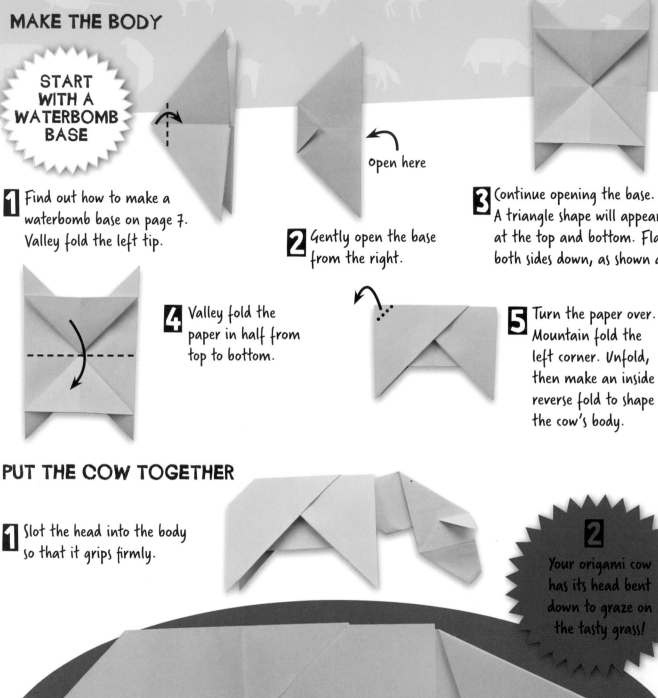

38

Wild animals

There's a huge variety of amazing creatures out there! Create your own wild world with this bunch of exciting origami animals, from a wily fox to a jumping frog!

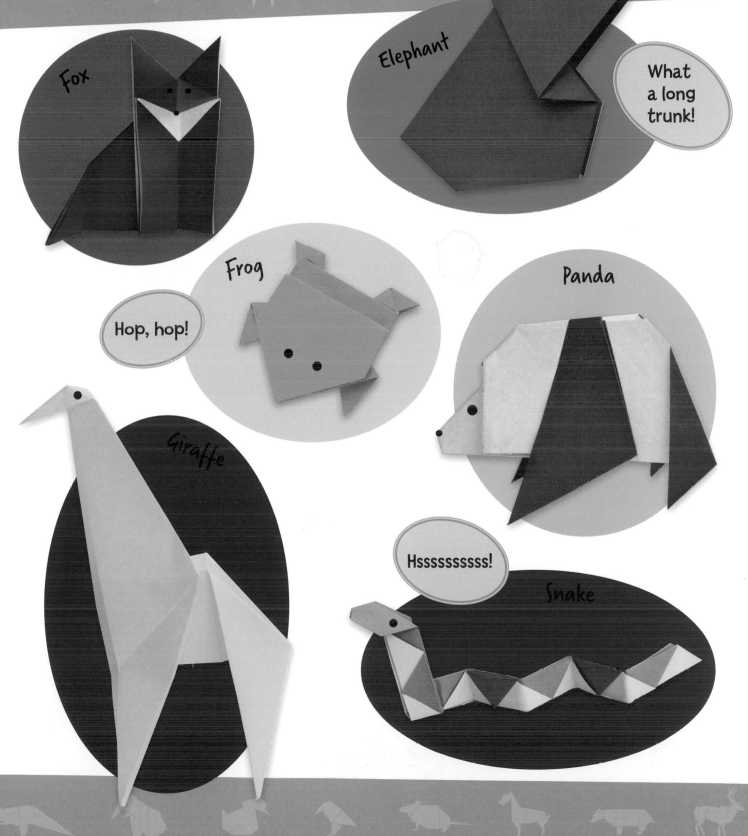

Fox

In many traditional stories, the fox is a symbol of trickery and cunning. You'll find that making this origami fox isn't too tricky, though!

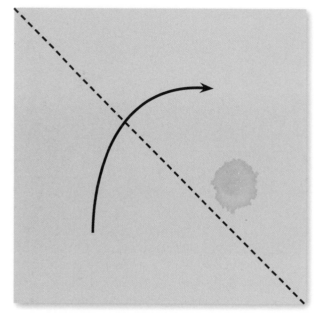

1 Start with a square of paper, white side up. Valley fold in half diagonally.

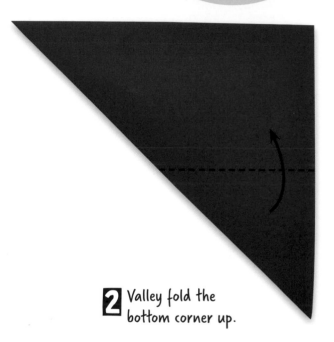

2 Valley fold the bottom corner up.

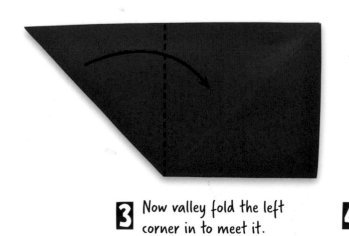

3 Now valley fold the left corner in to meet it.

4 Mountain fold the left section behind the right section.

5 Valley fold the right section.

Push

open out

6 Open out the right flap.

7 Push down the inside triangle to make a snout.

8 Valley fold the tail.

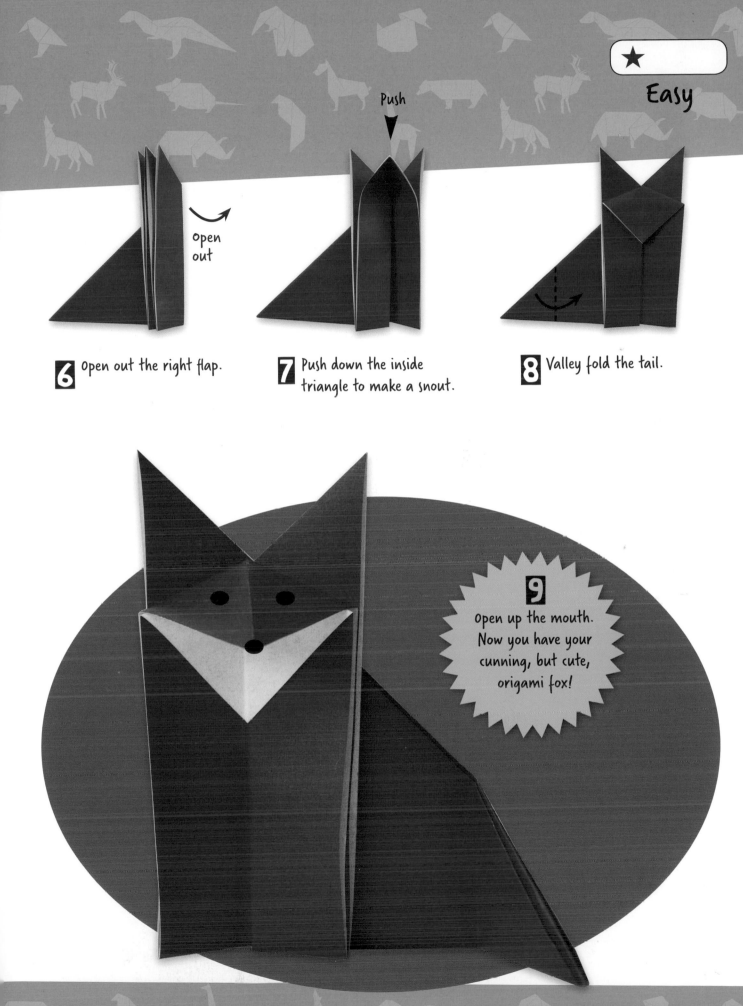

9
Open up the mouth. Now you have your cunning, but cute, origami fox!

Snake

Snakes don't have legs, so instead they use their strong muscles to pull themselves along the ground in a wavy motion.

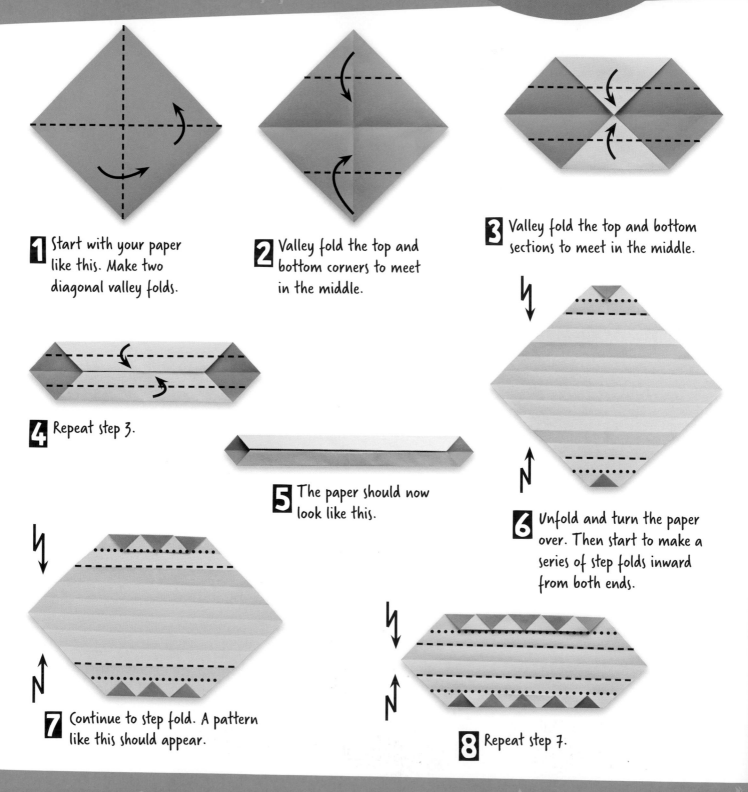

1 Start with your paper like this. Make two diagonal valley folds.

2 Valley fold the top and bottom corners to meet in the middle.

3 Valley fold the top and bottom sections to meet in the middle.

4 Repeat step 3.

5 The paper should now look like this.

6 Unfold and turn the paper over. Then start to make a series of step folds inward from both ends.

7 Continue to step fold. A pattern like this should appear.

8 Repeat step 7.

9 From the left, count in two and a half diamonds. Mountain fold the paper back on that line.

10 Unfold the last fold you made. Now mountain fold the bottom section back behind the top section.

Use this crease

11 Using the crease on the left that you made in step 9, make an outside reverse fold.

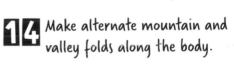

12 Mountain fold the top left corner.

13 Unfold, then make an outside reverse fold to create the snake's head.

14 Make alternate mountain and valley folds along the body.

15

Arrange the model like this. Now you have a zigzagging origami snake!

Panda

The panda is well-known for its striking black-and-white markings. Origami paper that is dark on one side and white on the other works really well for this model.

START WITH A WATERBOMB BASE

1 Find out how to make a waterbomb base on page 7. Make sure the white side is facing out. Valley fold the right flap.

2 Do the same on the other side.

Open up

3 Gently open up the flap on the right.

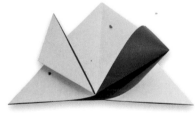

4 Make an outside reverse fold on this flap. Then do the same on the other side.

5 Valley fold the right tip of the bottom point.

6 Do the same on the other side.

Open up

7 Gently open up the bottom right flap.

8 Make an outside reverse fold. Then do the same on the other side.

9 Mountain fold the paper in half along the middle crease.

10 Turn the paper sideways, so that you now have the shape of the panda's body and legs. Mountain fold the top corner.

11 Unfold, then make an inside reverse fold to create the panda's back, as shown.

12 Step fold to make the panda's face.

13 Mountain fold the left point.

14 Unfold, then tuck the paper in to give the panda a blunt nose.

15 Open it out and stand it up to make a perfect origami panda!

Elephant

An elephant's trunk is strong and sensitive. It uses it for grasping food and sucking up water. Here's how to make an origami elephant with an impressive trunk!

START WITH A KITE BASE

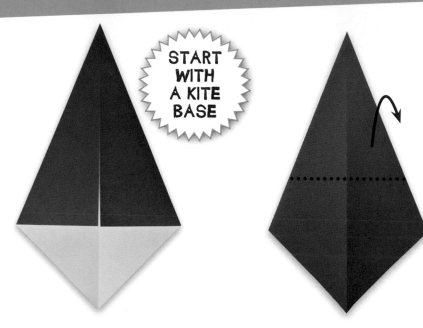

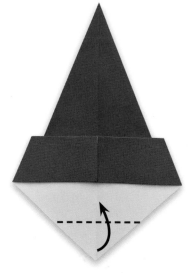

1 Find out how to make a kite base on page 6. Turn it upside down and turn the paper over.

2 Mountain fold the paper in half.

3 The paper should now look like this.

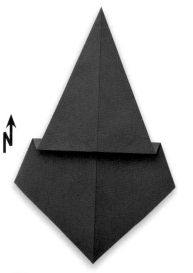

4 Open the paper out and then make a valley fold, to create a step fold as shown. Then turn the paper over.

5 Valley fold the bottom tip to meet the edge of the paper above.

6 The paper should now look like this.

Push

7 Turn the paper over. Mountain fold in half along the middle crease so that the right side folds behind the left.

8 Put your fingers inside the step fold on the left. Push back and down to change the angle of the point. This is the elephant's trunk.

9 Flatten the paper. Valley fold the top point.

10 Unfold, then make an outside reverse fold.

11 Valley fold the top point again. Unfold and make another outside reverse fold.

12 Turn the paper slightly to the left and open out the legs. You have a sitting origami elephant with a trumpeting trunk!

Giraffe

The giraffe has the longest neck of any animal on Earth. It uses its neck to help it reach juicy leaves at the tops of trees.

START WITH A BIRD BASE

1 Find out how to make a bird base on page 8. Position it so that the flaps with the open slit are on the left.

2 Take the right flap on the bottom layer and swing it round behind to the left, so that the two flaps are now in the middle as shown.

3 Take the left and right points, one in each hand, and gently pull the base open, so that it looks like this.

4 Continue pulling gently until the middle section starts to open like a bird's beak.

5 Open the paper slightly and make a mountain fold from the middle crease.

6 Close the paper again and press the left and right points together to make a star.

7 Bring the bottom point up to meet the top point. Flatten the paper.

8 Turn the paper over, so that the point is now facing down.

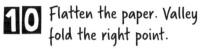

Push

9 Push the left point up and back so that the back flap goes behind, and the front flap swings round in front.

10 Flatten the paper. Valley fold the right point.

11 Unfold, then make an outside reverse fold to create the giraffe's back legs.

12 Valley fold the top point.

14 Stand up your origami giraffe and show off that incredible neck!

13 Unfold, then do an outside reverse fold to create the giraffe's head.

Jumping frog

Frogs move by jumping on their strong back legs. Here's how to make an origami frog which can spring into action!

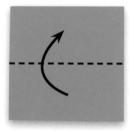

1 Start with a square of paper, white side up. Valley fold it in half from left to right.

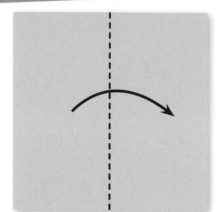

2 Valley fold it in half again by bringing the top section down.

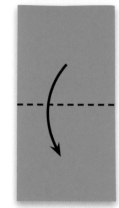

3 Valley fold the flap on the top layer to meet the top edge of the paper.

4 The paper should now look like this.

5 Unfold the last two steps. Valley fold the top right corner.

6 Unfold, then valley fold the top left corner.

7 The paper should now look like this.

8 Unfold the top section of the paper.

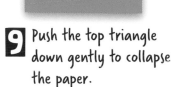

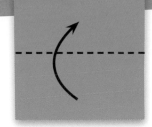

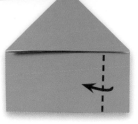

9 Push the top triangle down gently to collapse the paper.

10 Flatten down the paper at the top to make a triangle. Valley fold the bottom section to meet the edge of the triangle.

11 Take the bottom flap on the right and valley fold it to meet the middle, so that it sits beneath the triangle.

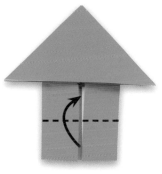

12 Do the same on the other side.

13 Valley fold the bottom section to meet the edge of the triangle.

14 Valley fold both bottom corners.

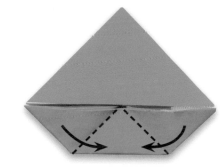

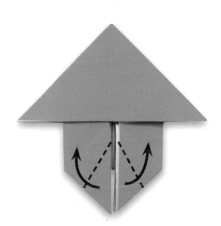

15 Unfold the bottom sections. Poke in the top corners to make a boat shape, as shown in step 16.

16 Flatten the paper. Valley fold the bottom right corner. Do the same on the other side.

17 Valley fold the bottom right corner again, the other way. Do the same on the other side.

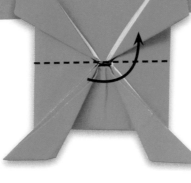

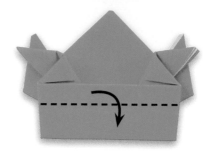

18 Now valley fold the top right corner. Do the same on the other side.

19 Valley fold the paper in half along the middle crease.

20 Valley fold the top section down. The fold is very tight!

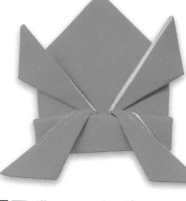

21 The paper should now look like this.

22 Turn the paper over and you have an origami frog. Push your finger down on the fold at the back to see it spring!

Pets

Is there a pet that you've always wanted to own? Why not make yourself an origami version? There's plenty to choose from here, from a cool cat to a swimming turtle!

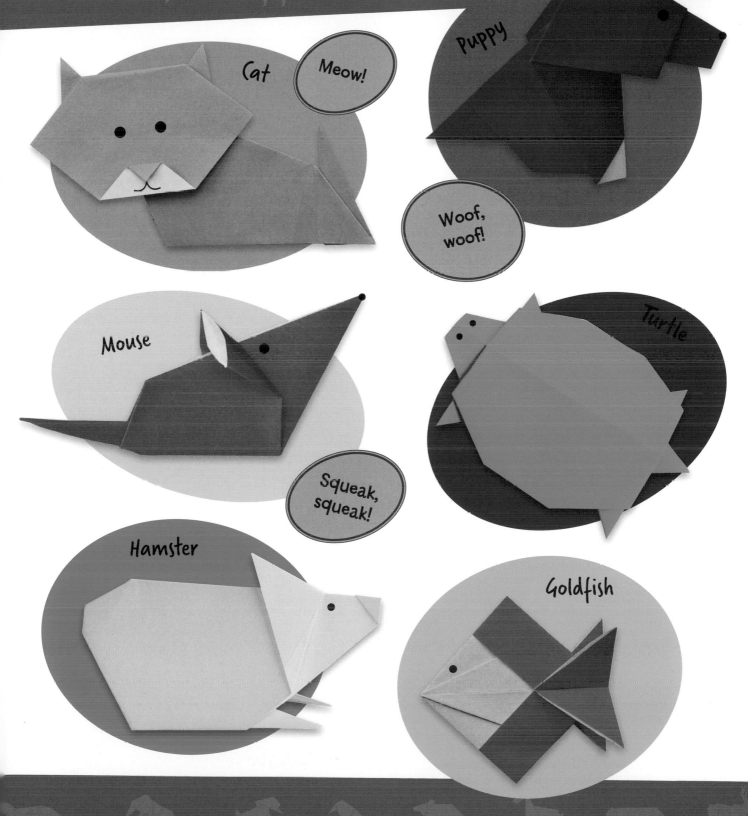

Cat

Cats have lived with people as pets for thousands of years. The cat makes a good companion as it's friendly and loves to sit on laps!

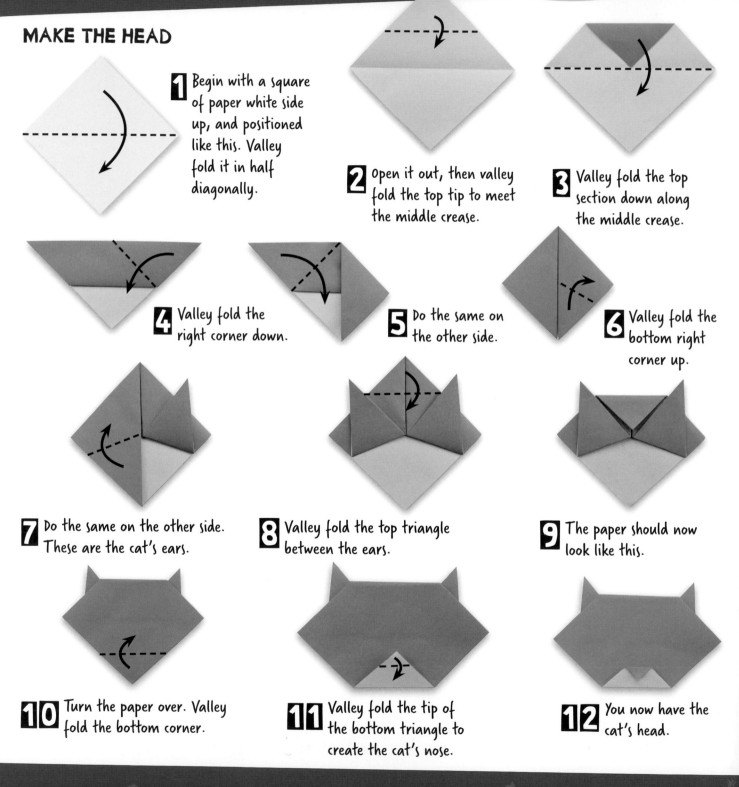

MAKE THE HEAD

1 Begin with a square of paper white side up, and positioned like this. Valley fold it in half diagonally.

2 Open it out, then valley fold the top tip to meet the middle crease.

3 Valley fold the top section down along the middle crease.

4 Valley fold the right corner down.

5 Do the same on the other side.

6 Valley fold the bottom right corner up.

7 Do the same on the other side. These are the cat's ears.

8 Valley fold the top triangle between the ears.

9 The paper should now look like this.

10 Turn the paper over. Valley fold the bottom corner.

11 Valley fold the tip of the bottom triangle to create the cat's nose.

12 You now have the cat's head.

MAKE THE BODY

START WITH A KITE BASE

★ **Easy**

1 Find out how to make a kite base on page 6. Turn it on its side, as shown. Valley fold in half.

2 Valley fold the right point.

3 Valley fold the right corner.

4 The paper should now look like this.

5 Open up the folds you made in steps 2 and 3.

Open out

6 Gently lift the right corner and open it out.

7 Flatten the paper down into a kite shape as shown. Valley fold the bottom triangle.

8 Valley fold the left flap of the triangle over to the right to create the cat's tail.

9 You now have the cat's body, as shown above.

PUT THE CAT TOGETHER

1 Balance the head on the top point of the cat's body.

2 Now fold out the back legs — and you have an origami cat to make friends with!

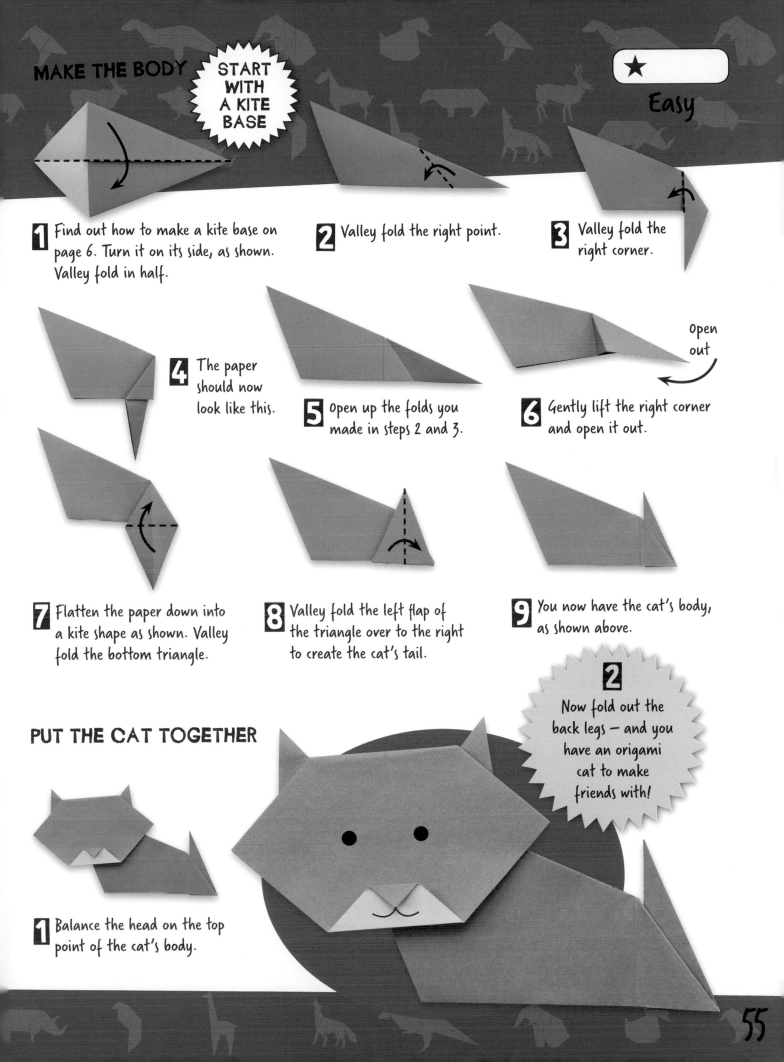

55

Hamster

The hamster carries food in special pouches in its cheeks. When the pouches are full, the hamster's face can look enormous!

1 Start with a square of paper in this position, white side up. Valley fold it in half diagonally.

2 Open the paper and valley fold it in half diagonally the other way.

3 Turn the paper, so that the point is upward, as shown. Valley fold the tip of the top flap.

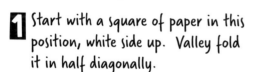

4 Valley fold the tip of the flap underneath.

5 The paper should now look like this. Turn the paper over.

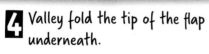

6 Valley fold the right corner to make a flap.

7 Do the same on the other side.

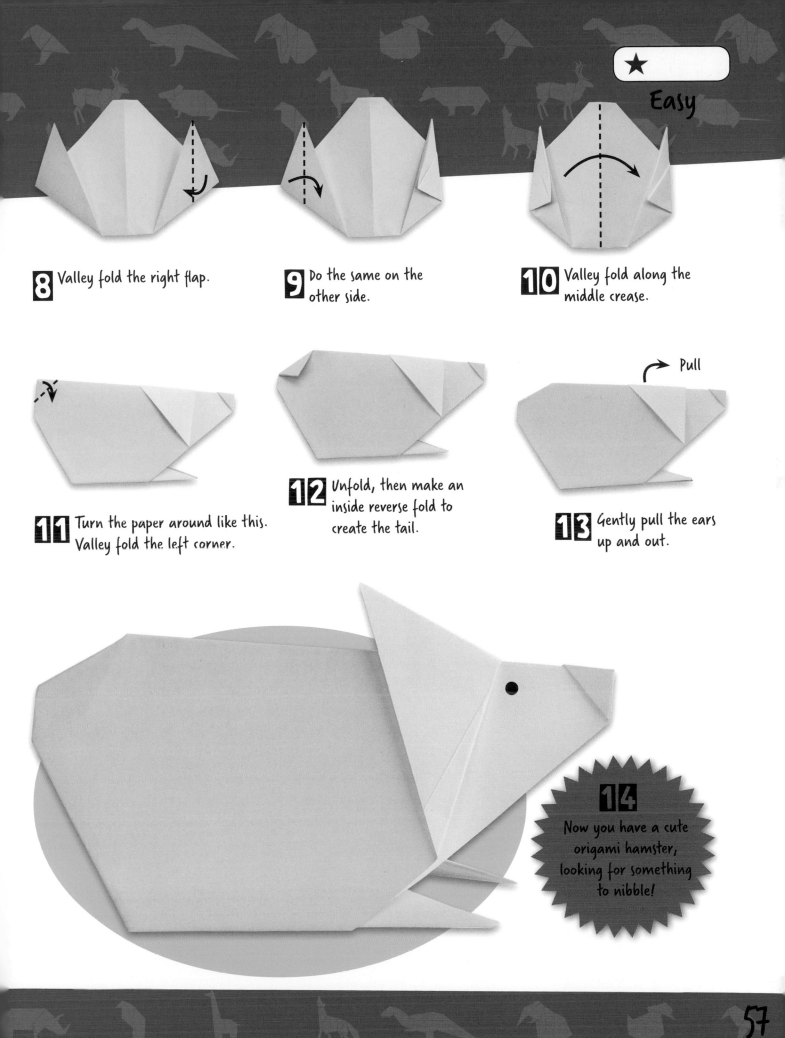

8 Valley fold the right flap.

9 Do the same on the other side.

10 Valley fold along the middle crease.

11 Turn the paper around like this. Valley fold the left corner.

12 Unfold, then make an inside reverse fold to create the tail.

Pull

13 Gently pull the ears up and out.

14 Now you have a cute origami hamster, looking for something to nibble!

Puppy

Puppies are bouncy and playful, but they have to be trained to do what they're told! Here's a fun origami puppy, just for you.

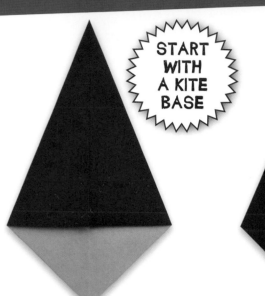

START WITH A KITE BASE

1 Find out how to make a kite base on page 6. Turn it upside down. Turn the paper over.

2 Mountain fold it in half so that the top section goes behind the bottom section.

3 The paper should now look like this. Unfold.

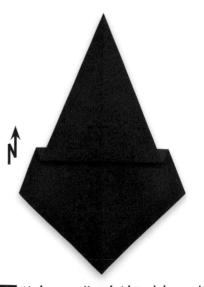

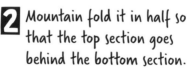

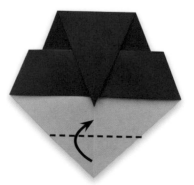

4 Make a valley fold just beneath the crease to make a step fold. Turn the paper over.

5 Valley fold the top point.

6 Valley fold the bottom point up to meet the tip of the top section.

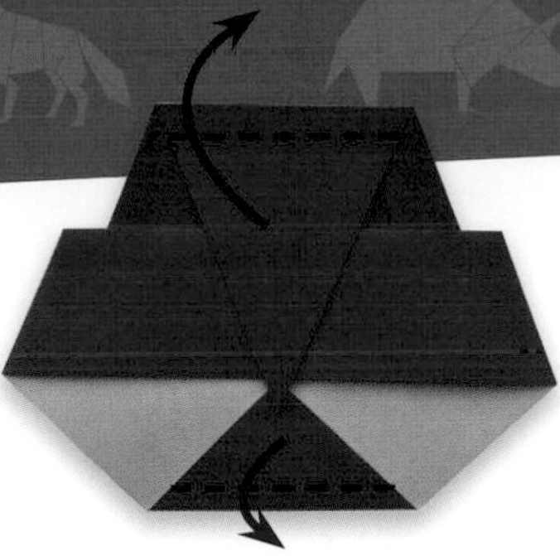

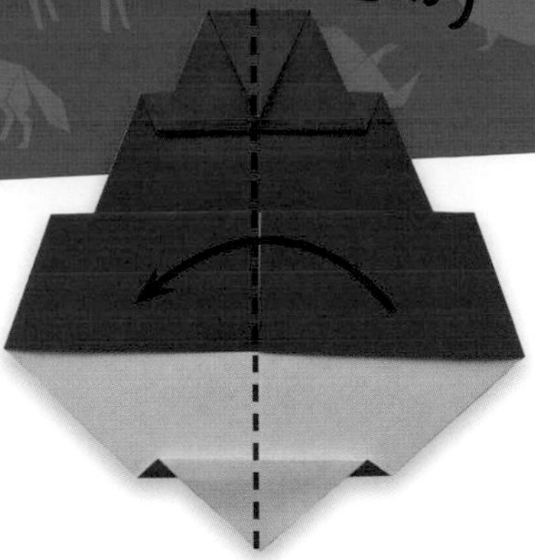

7 Valley fold the top section up and the bottom section down.

8 Fold the top tip down in a valley fold.

9 Valley fold the paper in half along the middle crease from right to left.

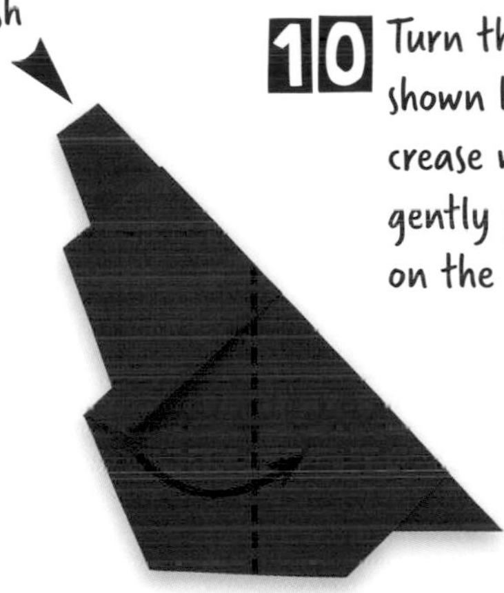

Push

10 Turn the paper round, as shown here. Valley fold and crease well. Unfold, then gently push down and back on the puppy's nose.

11 As you push, the flaps pop back into place, revealing the puppy's white feet.

12
Stand up your origami model and you have a perfectly cute, puppy playmate!

Goldfish

Although they're called goldfish, these fish actually come in many varieties, including red, orange, yellow, white, black, and brown. Make yours a bright one!

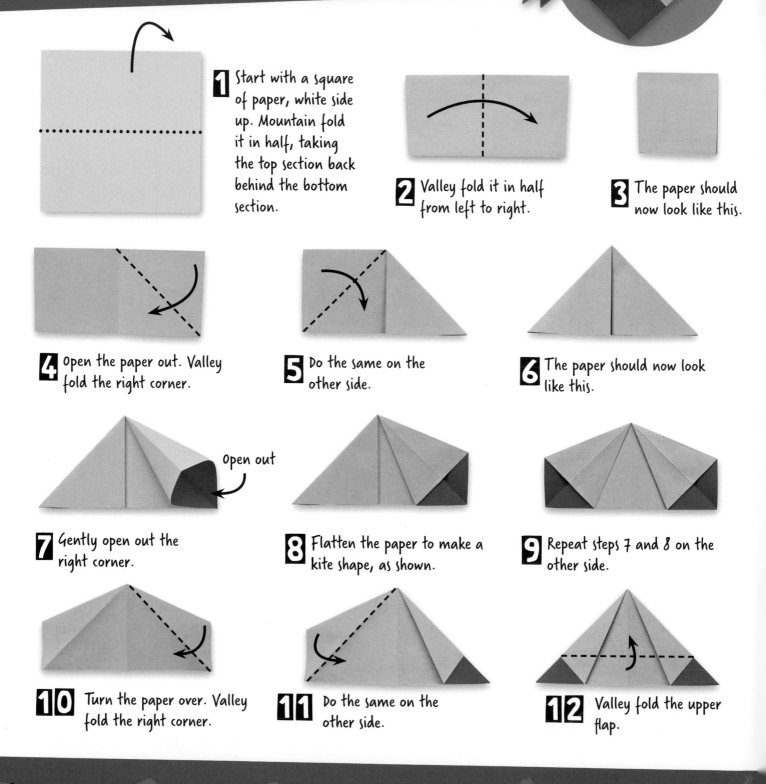

1 Start with a square of paper, white side up. Mountain fold it in half, taking the top section back behind the bottom section.

2 Valley fold it in half from left to right.

3 The paper should now look like this.

4 Open the paper out. Valley fold the right corner.

5 Do the same on the other side.

6 The paper should now look like this.

Open out

7 Gently open out the right corner.

8 Flatten the paper to make a kite shape, as shown.

9 Repeat steps 7 and 8 on the other side.

10 Turn the paper over. Valley fold the right corner.

11 Do the same on the other side.

12 Valley fold the upper flap.

13 The paper should now look like this. Turn it over.

14 Valley fold the bottom section.

15 Valley fold the right upper flap.

16 Do the same on the other side.

17 Mountain fold the right and left corners at the back.

Open up

18 The paper should now look like this. Start to open the bottom out.

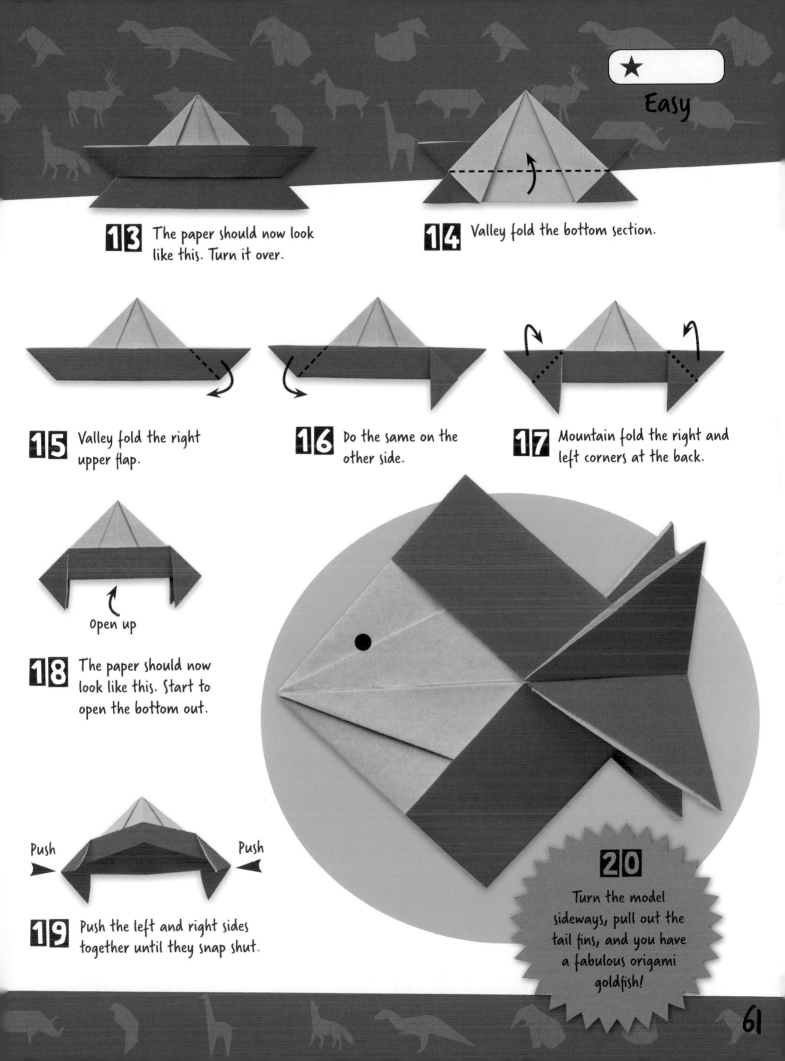

Push   Push

19 Push the left and right sides together until they snap shut.

20 Turn the model sideways, pull out the tail fins, and you have a fabulous origami goldfish!

Mouse

The mouse has an excellent sense of smell and it investigates its surroundings with a long, pointy nose – just like this origami version!

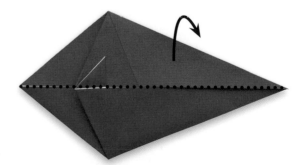

START WITH A FISH BASE

1 Find out how to make a fish base on page 6. Turn it so that the flaps are pointing to the left. Mountain fold the bottom flap and tuck it under itself.

2 Mountain fold the top flap and tuck it under the bottom flap.

3 Mountain fold the left point.

4 Mountain fold the top left corner.

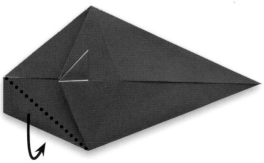

5 Do the same on the other side.

6 Mountain fold in half, so that the top section folds down behind the bottom section.

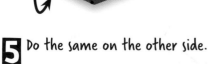

7 Valley fold the front flap. Then do the same to the back flap to create the ears.

8 Mountain fold the right point and then valley fold to make a step fold.

9 Unfold and do an inside reverse fold to make the tail point down, as shown. Then do a second inside reverse fold to tuck the tail back up.

Pull

10 Mountain fold the right edge of the front flap of the tail to tuck it in and make it narrow. Do the same for the back flap.

11 Open out the ears and pull the tail down gently.

12 You now have an inquisitive origami mouse, complete with a pointy nose and tail!

Turtle

The turtle spends a lot of time in water. It has powerful flippers to help it swim. It also has a hard, rounded shell to protect it from predators.

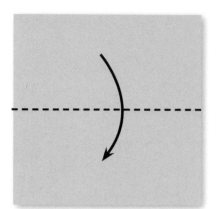

1 Start with your paper white side up. Valley fold it in half and open it out.

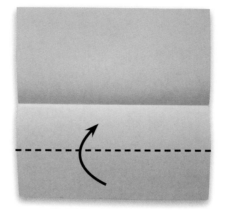

2 Valley fold the bottom section up to the middle crease.

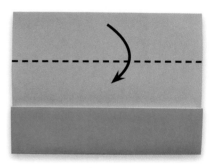

3 Do the same for the top section.

4 Valley fold the right corner.

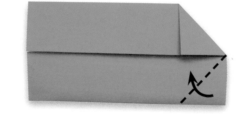

5 Do the same on the other side.

6 The paper should now look like this.

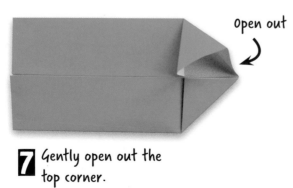

Open out

7 Gently open out the top corner.

8 Flatten the paper to make a triangle shape as shown.

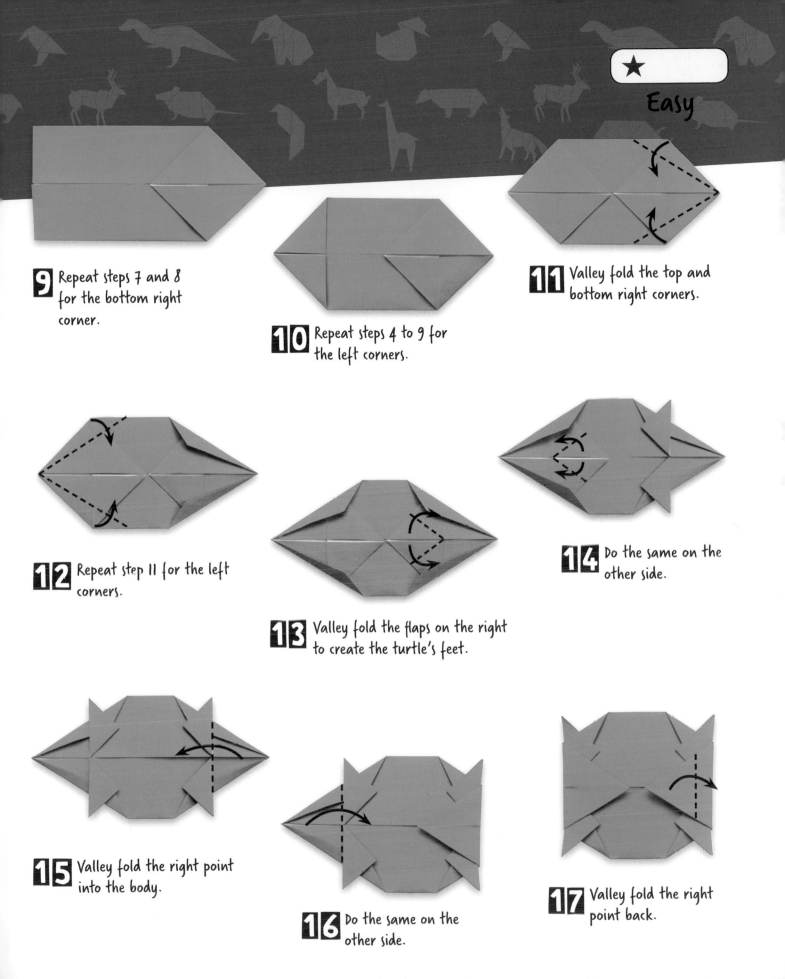

9 Repeat steps 7 and 8 for the bottom right corner.

10 Repeat steps 4 to 9 for the left corners.

11 Valley fold the top and bottom right corners.

12 Repeat step 11 for the left corners.

13 Valley fold the flaps on the right to create the turtle's feet.

14 Do the same on the other side.

15 Valley fold the right point into the body.

16 Do the same on the other side.

17 Valley fold the right point back.

Turtle... continued

18 Do the same on the other side.

19 Valley fold the left tip. This is the turtle's nose.

20 Turn the paper over. Bend it slightly along the middle crease.

21 Now stand your origami turtle up on its claws. It's ready for a dip in the water!

Birds and butterflies

Find out how to make a variety of beautiful birds and even a pretty butterfly. Your origami models will look as if they are ready to take flight!

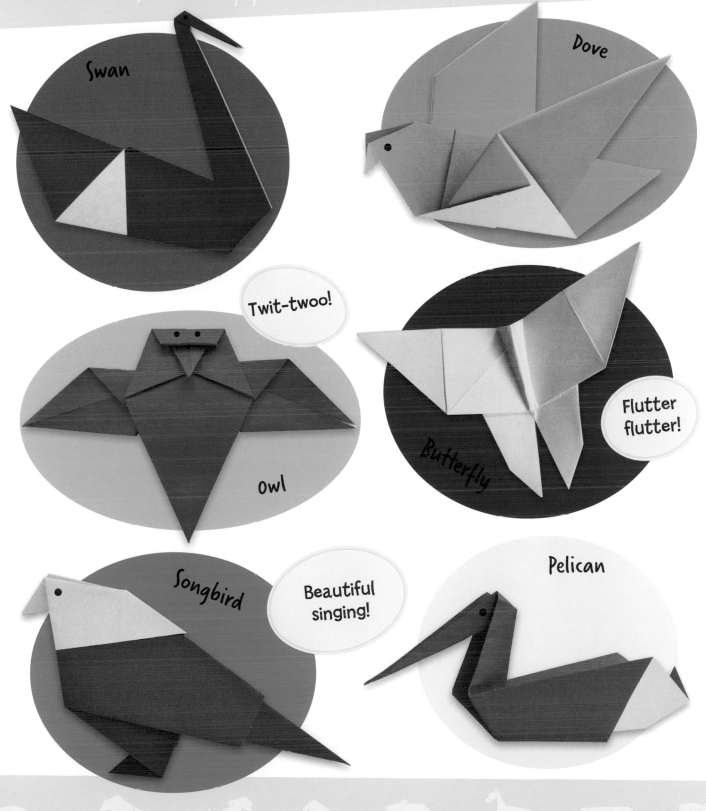

Swan

Dove

Twit-twoo!

Owl

Flutter flutter!

Butterfly

Songbird

Beautiful singing!

Pelican

Swan

There are few more elegant sights than a graceful swan gliding across a lake. Here's how to make one.

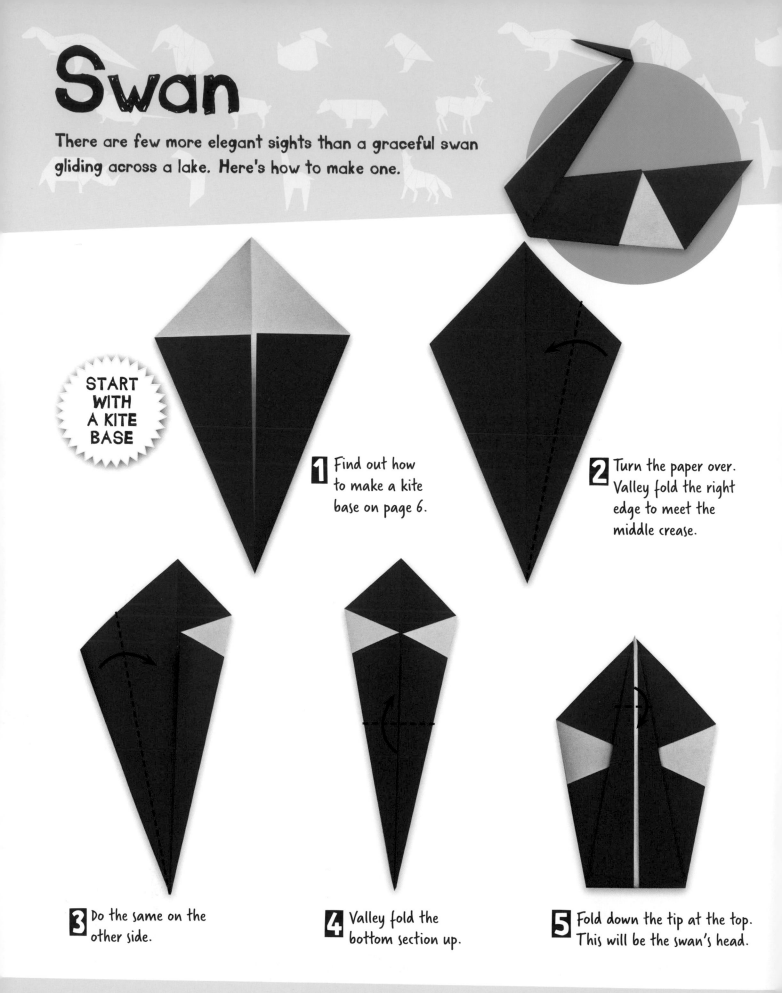

START WITH A KITE BASE

1 Find out how to make a kite base on page 6.

2 Turn the paper over. Valley fold the right edge to meet the middle crease.

3 Do the same on the other side.

4 Valley fold the bottom section up.

5 Fold down the tip at the top. This will be the swan's head.

6 Mountain fold along the middle crease so that the left side folds behind the right.

Pull

7 Now turn your paper sideways so that it looks like this. Pull up the neck as shown.

Pull

8 Flatten the paper and then pull the head into position.

9 Now you have a beautiful swan. Try placing it on water and see if it floats!

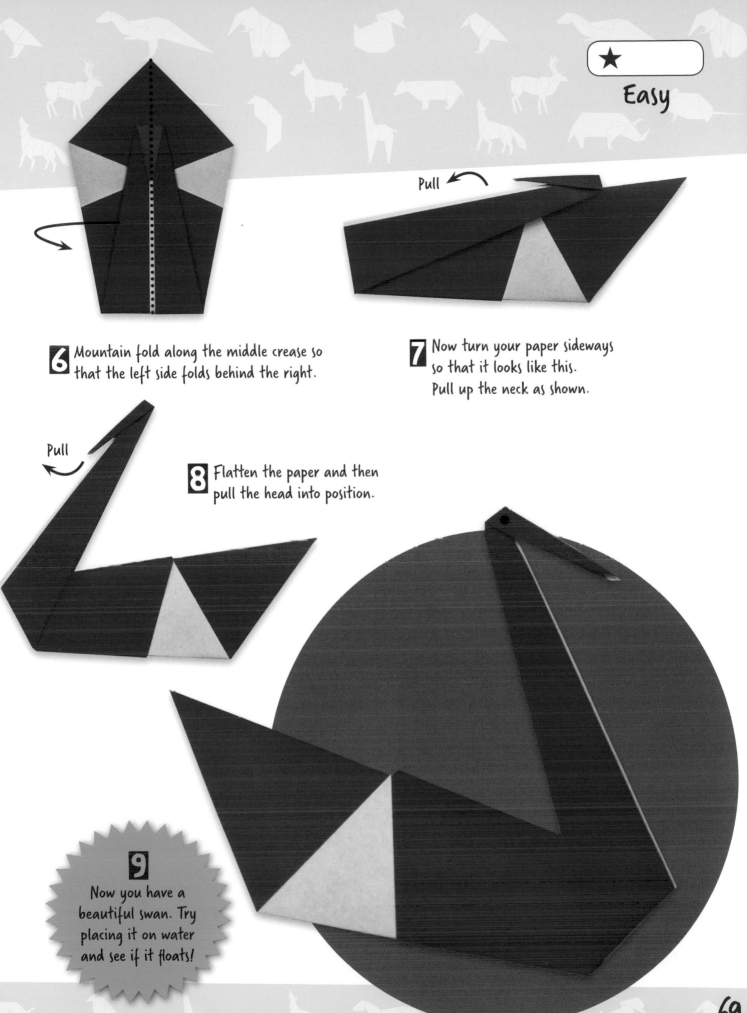

Pelican

The pelican has an extremely long beak which it uses to scoop up fish and other small creatures to eat. Gulp!

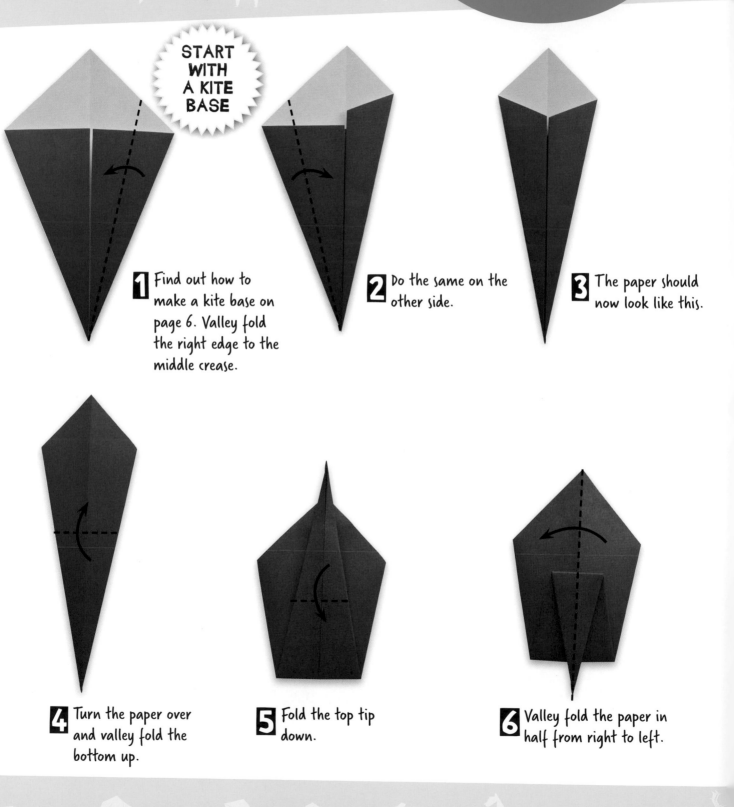

START WITH A KITE BASE

1 Find out how to make a kite base on page 6. Valley fold the right edge to the middle crease.

2 Do the same on the other side.

3 The paper should now look like this.

4 Turn the paper over and valley fold the bottom up.

5 Fold the top tip down.

6 Valley fold the paper in half from right to left.

7 Turn the paper sideways, so that the tip points out to the left as shown.

8 Gently pull the neck of the pelican from inside so that it sits upright. Mountain fold the tail.

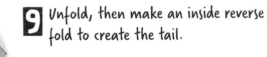

9 Unfold, then make an inside reverse fold to create the tail.

10 You now have a perfectly poised pelican ready to go and catch some fish with that huge beak!

Dove

The dove is traditionally used as a symbol of peace and love. Make your own peace symbol with this origami version!

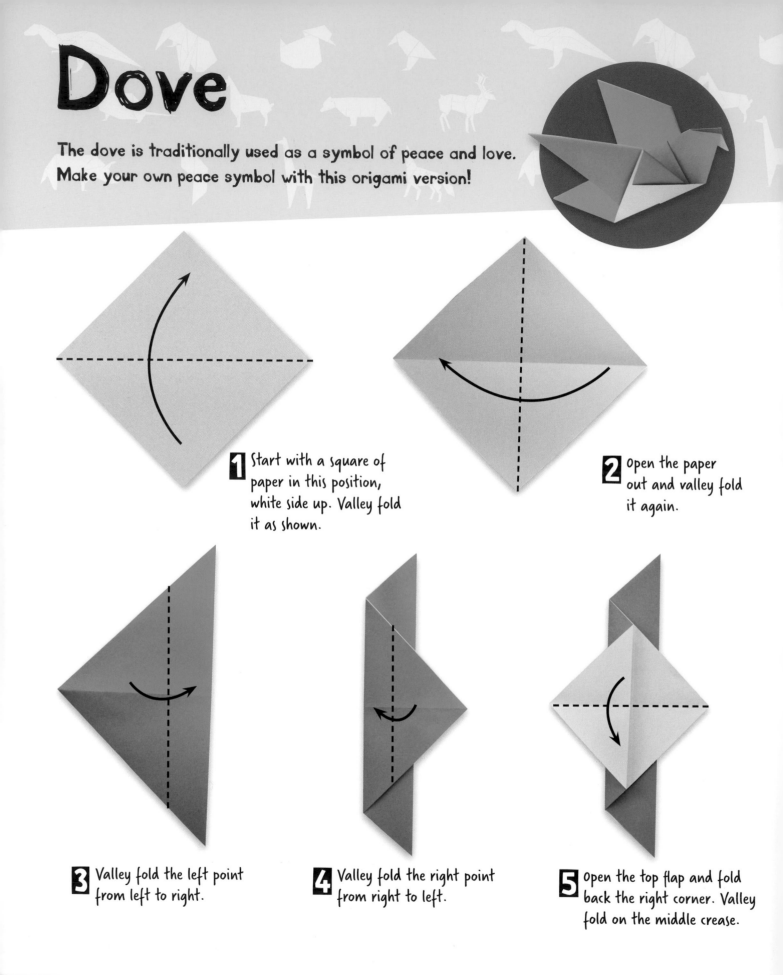

1 Start with a square of paper in this position, white side up. Valley fold it as shown.

2 Open the paper out and valley fold it again.

3 Valley fold the left point from left to right.

4 Valley fold the right point from right to left.

5 Open the top flap and fold back the right corner. Valley fold on the middle crease.

6 Fold the top flap up to make a wing. Do the same on the other side.

7 Mountain fold the left tip.

8 Unfold, then make an inside reverse fold to create the beak.

9 Gently pull out the wings and your origami dove is ready to take to the air!

Songbird

Many different types of small birds can be found in gardens and parks. Here's how to make the origami kind!

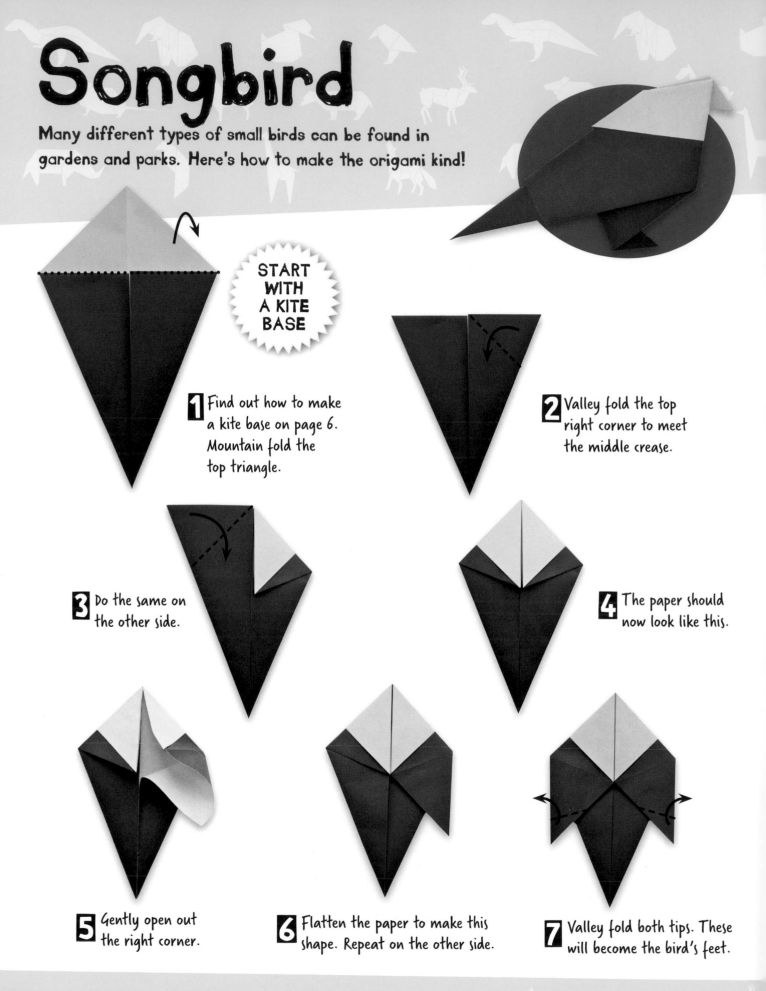

START WITH A KITE BASE

1 Find out how to make a kite base on page 6. Mountain fold the top triangle.

2 Valley fold the top right corner to meet the middle crease.

3 Do the same on the other side.

4 The paper should now look like this.

5 Gently open out the right corner.

6 Flatten the paper to make this shape. Repeat on the other side.

7 Valley fold both tips. These will become the bird's feet.

74

8 Valley fold the paper in half along the middle crease, from right to left.

9 Step fold the lower point. Unfold, then tuck the tail in and then out again along the fold lines. Valley fold the top point.

10 Turn the paper sideways. Unfold, then make an inside reverse fold to create the head.

11 This is what your songbird should look like from above.

12 Stand your model up on its feet. Your origami bird now looks ready to burst into song!

Owl

The owl is often used as a symbol of wisdom and knowledge. Your origami owl looks powerful and alert as it opens its wings wide.

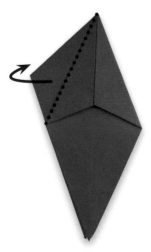

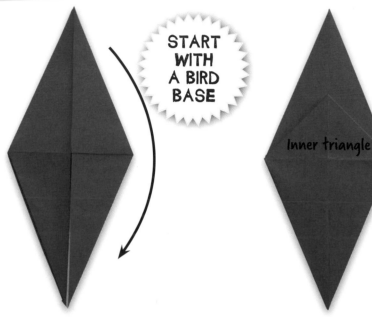

START WITH A BIRD BASE

1 Find out how to make a bird base on page 8. With the two open flaps pointing down, fold the upper top flap down to meet the bottom tip.

2 The inner triangle should now be revealed, as shown above.

Inner triangle

3 Turn the paper over and repeat step 2 so that the inner triangle sticks up. Valley fold the right corner to the middle crease.

4 Do the same on the other side.

5 Mountain fold the right corner so that it folds back.

6 Do the same on the other side.

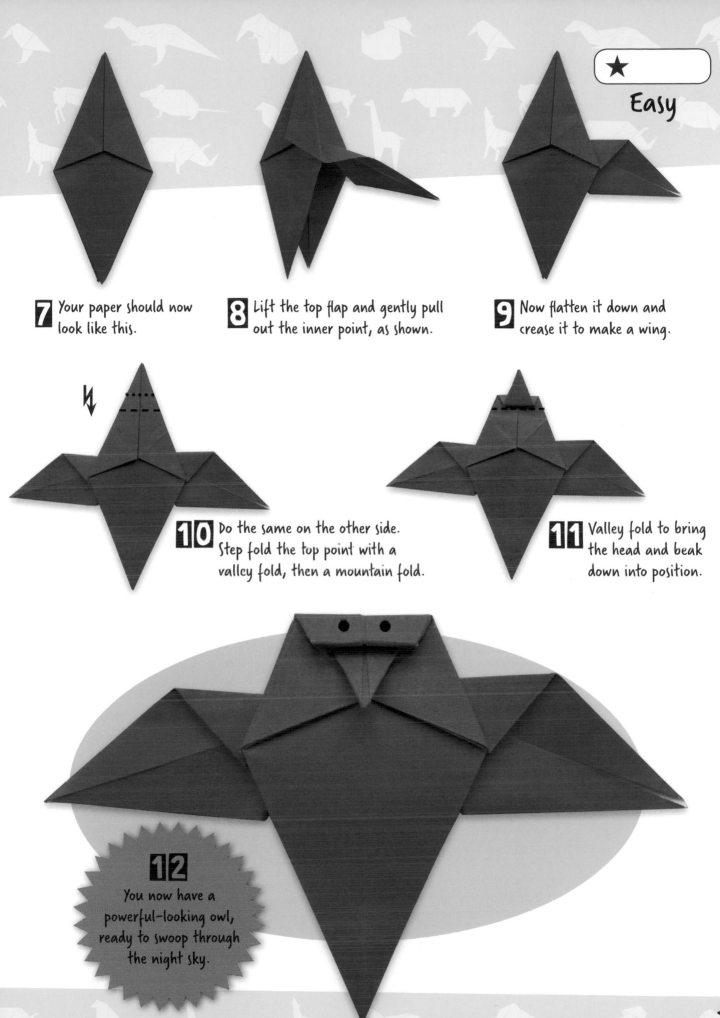

7 Your paper should now look like this.

8 Lift the top flap and gently pull out the inner point, as shown.

9 Now flatten it down and crease it to make a wing.

10 Do the same on the other side. Step fold the top point with a valley fold, then a mountain fold.

11 Valley fold to bring the head and beak down into position.

12 You now have a powerful-looking owl, ready to swoop through the night sky.

Butterfly

A butterfly has four wings and the patterns on the right side are symmetrical with the patterns on the left. You could decorate yours after you've made it!

1 Start with the paper white side up. Valley fold it in half and open it up. Then valley fold it in half the other way and open it again.

2 Valley fold the paper diagonally and open it up. Fold it diagonally the other way and open it again.

3 Valley fold the top right corner. Fold the other corners in the same way.

4 Valley fold the top right corner again.

5 Fold the other corners in the same way.

6 You should now have a small square, like this.

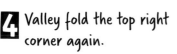

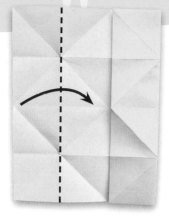

7 Unfold your paper completely. Valley fold the right section.

8 Valley fold the left section to meet in the middle.

9 Your paper should now look like this.

10 Take the top corners and gently pull them open, so that the top folds down.

11 Keep pulling the corners out and bringing the top down, so that this shape appears.

12 Flatten the paper as shown. Then turn it so that the top becomes the bottom.

13 Repeat steps 10 and 11 to get the shape in this picture. Mountain fold the top section back.

14 Valley fold the upper right flap.

15 Do the same on the other side.

Butterfly... continued

16 Valley fold the right upper right flap.

17 Do the same on the other side.

18 Valley fold the paper in half from left to right.

19 Mountain fold the top left corner.

20 Unfold, then open out the butterfly. Pinch the fold you just made in step 19 to create the butterfly's body.

21 Push back the right wing to shape the body.

22 Pinch the body so that it sticks out. Now your origami butterfly is ready to flutter!

Dinosaurs

The dinosaurs lived millions of years ago. They weren't all big and fierce – they came in lots of different shapes and sizes. Check out these origami ones, from the terrible T. rex to the giant Diplodocus!

Baby Maiasaura

Allosaurus

Diplodocus

Plesiosaurus

Splish, splash!

Spiky plates!

Stegosaurus

T. rex

ROAR!

Baby Maiasaura

Maiasaura means "good mother lizard" because this dinosaur cared for its young and protected them from danger. Here's how to make one of Maiasaura's babies!

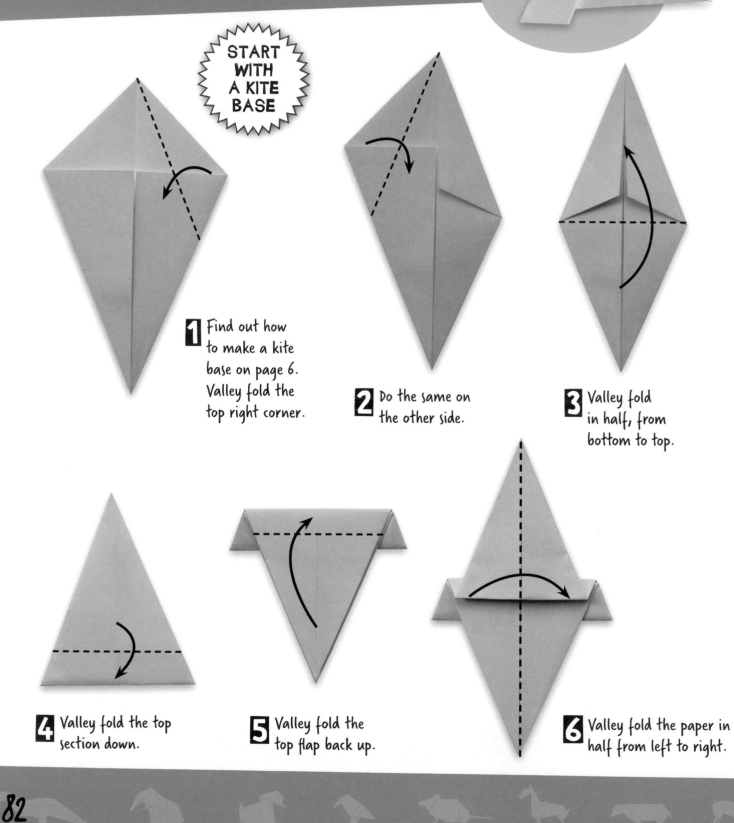

START WITH A KITE BASE

1 Find out how to make a kite base on page 6. Valley fold the top right corner.

2 Do the same on the other side.

3 Valley fold in half, from bottom to top.

4 Valley fold the top section down.

5 Valley fold the top flap back up.

6 Valley fold the paper in half from left to right.

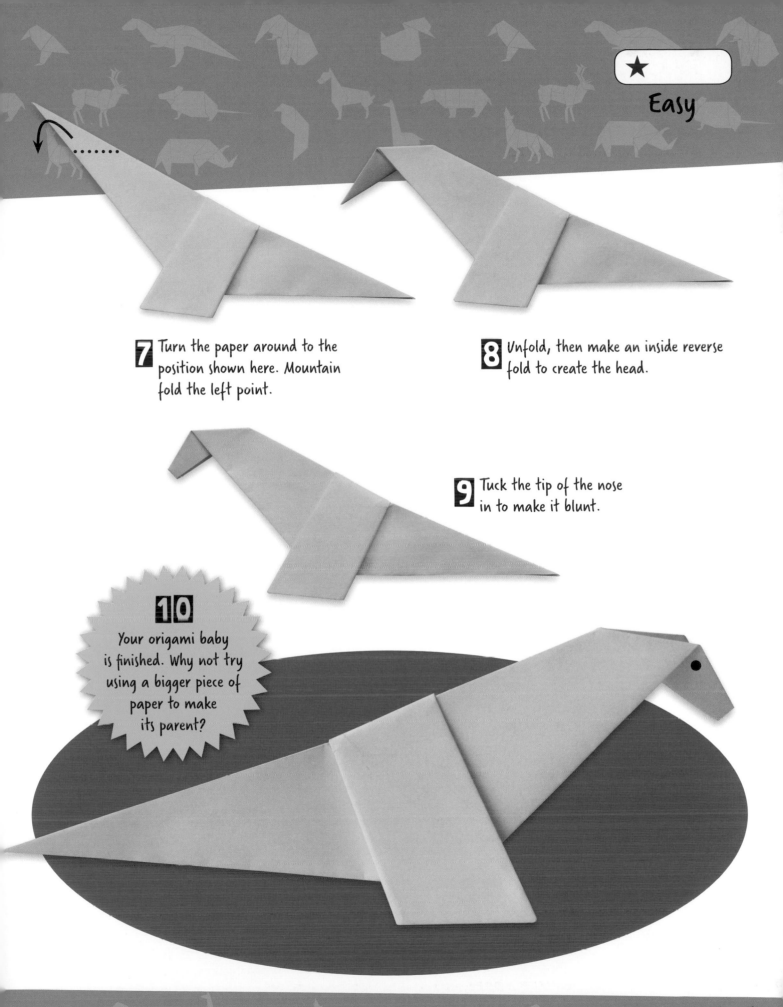

7 Turn the paper around to the position shown here. Mountain fold the left point.

8 Unfold, then make an inside reverse fold to create the head.

9 Tuck the tip of the nose in to make it blunt.

10 Your origami baby is finished. Why not try using a bigger piece of paper to make its parent?

Diplodocus

The Diplodocus was a **huge plant-eating dinosaur**. It may have used its long, powerful tail like a whip to strike at its enemies.

START WITH A KITE BASE

1 Find out how to make a kite base on page 6, starting with the white side facing down. Turn it on its side, as shown.

2 Turn the paper over. Valley fold the top section to the middle.

3 Do the same on the other side.

Unfold

4 Unfold the upper flap on both sides.

5 Refold both flaps into valley folds.

6 The paper should now look like this.

Open

7 Gently lift the corner of the top flap and open it out.

8 Now flatten the paper to form a triangle as shown.

9 Do the same on the other side.

Open

10 Gently open out the left corner.

11 Flatten the paper into a triangle as shown, so that it slightly overlaps the triangle you made in step 8.

12 Do the same on the other side. Mountain fold in half, so that the bottom folds behind the top.

13 The flaps should point to the right. Fold the two flaps back to form the legs. Do the same on both sides.

14 Valley fold the right point so that it goes straight up.

15 Unfold, then make an inside reverse fold to create the neck.

16 Flatten the paper.

17 Mountain fold the right point.

18 Unfold, then make an inside reverse fold to create the head.

20 Stand up your cute origami Diplodocus — but watch out for that whipping tail!

19 Flatten the head and angle it a little bit. Tuck in the tip of the nose to make it blunt.

Plesiosaurus

When dinosaurs were roaming the Earth, giant long-necked reptiles called plesiosaurs swam in the oceans. This one is called Plesiosaurus.

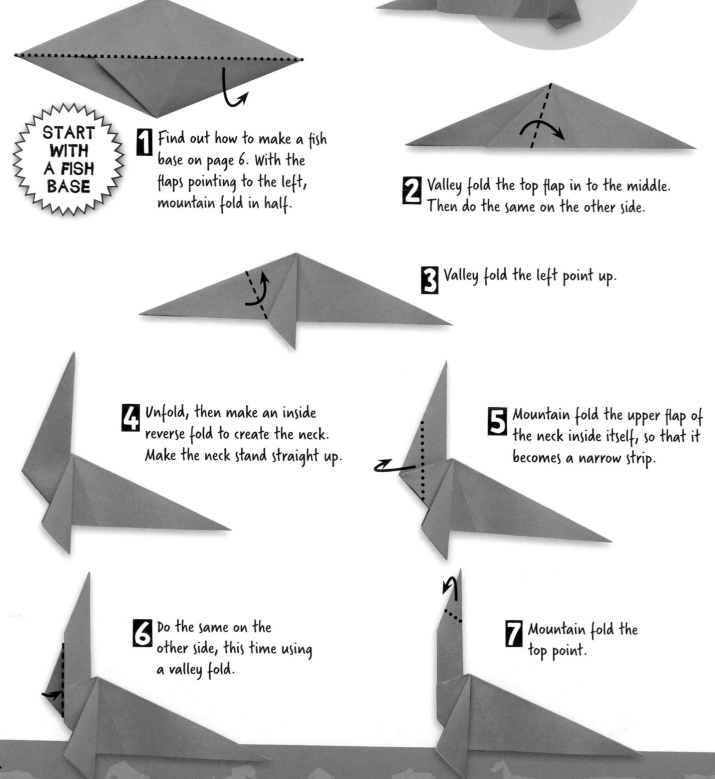

START WITH A FISH BASE

1 Find out how to make a fish base on page 6. With the flaps pointing to the left, mountain fold in half.

2 Valley fold the top flap in to the middle. Then do the same on the other side.

3 Valley fold the left point up.

4 Unfold, then make an inside reverse fold to create the neck. Make the neck stand straight up.

5 Mountain fold the upper flap of the neck inside itself, so that it becomes a narrow strip.

6 Do the same on the other side, this time using a valley fold.

7 Mountain fold the top point.

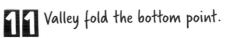

8 Unfold, then make an inside reverse fold to create the head. Flatten it and angle it.

9 Tuck in the end of the nose. Then mountain fold and valley fold the tail to make a step fold.

10 Unfold, then tuck the tail in and then out again along the fold lines.

11 Valley fold the bottom point.

12 Do the same on the other side to create two flippers.

13 Balance the Plesiosaurus on its flippers. And now you have an origami prehistoric sea monster!

Allosaurus

Allosaurus was rather like its more famous cousin, T. rex. Although it wasn't quite as big in length or height, it was still a fearsome fighter!

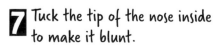

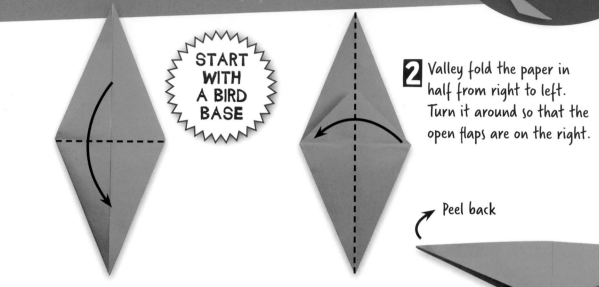

START WITH A BIRD BASE

1 Find out how to make a bird base on page 8, and then place your paper like this. Valley fold the front flap.

2 Valley fold the paper in half from right to left. Turn it around so that the open flaps are on the right.

Peel back

3 Peel back the left flap to reveal the triangle underneath, as shown in step 4.

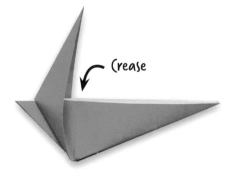

Crease

4 The edge of the upright piece should meet the crease on the body. Flatten the paper.

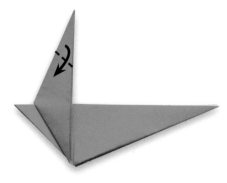

5 Valley fold the top point.

6 Unfold, then make an outside reverse fold to create the head.

7 Tuck the tip of the nose inside to make it blunt.

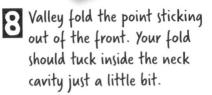

8 Valley fold the point sticking out of the front. Your fold should tuck inside the neck cavity just a little bit.

9 Unfold, then make an inside reverse fold to create the arms.

10 Valley fold the top flap down to create a leg. Do the same on the other side.

11 Valley fold the bottom tip of the leg to create a foot.

12 Do the same on the other side.

13
Your fierce origami Allosaurus should now balance on its feet. Watch out, dinosaurs!

Stegosaurus

Stegosaurus had two rows of spiky plates running along its back. They were used to help it keep warm – it turned them to the sun to warm up.

MAKE THE HEAD AND BODY

1 Turn your paper white side up. Valley fold in half and unfold.

2 Valley fold the right section to the middle crease.

3 Do the same on the other side.

4 Valley fold the top right corner.

5 Do the same on the other side.

6 Repeat steps 4 and 5 for the bottom corners.

7 Unfold all the corners so that the paper looks like this.

8 Open out the top right corner and make an inside reverse fold.

90

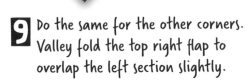

9 Do the same for the other corners. Valley fold the top right flap to overlap the left section slightly.

10 Valley fold the top left flap to overlap the right flap.

11 Repeat steps 9 and 10 for the bottom flaps.

12 The paper should now look like this. Turn the paper over.

13 Valley fold the top edges.

14 Valley fold the right and left corners to meet in the middle.

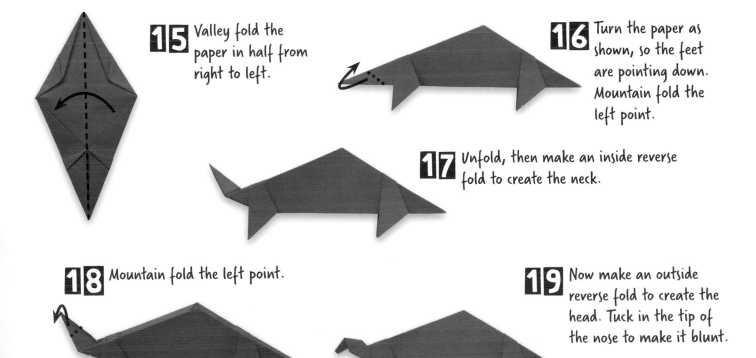

15 Valley fold the paper in half from right to left.

16 Turn the paper as shown, so the feet are pointing down. Mountain fold the left point.

17 Unfold, then make an inside reverse fold to create the neck.

18 Mountain fold the left point.

19 Now make an outside reverse fold to create the head. Tuck in the tip of the nose to make it blunt.

MAKE THE BACK

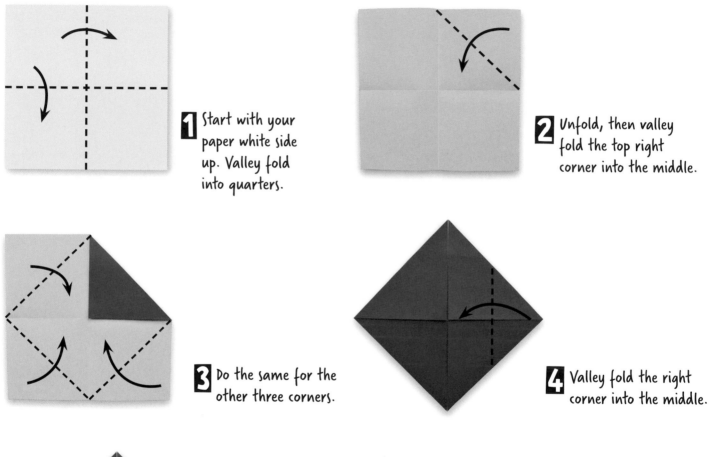

1 Start with your paper white side up. Valley fold into quarters.

2 Unfold, then valley fold the top right corner into the middle.

3 Do the same for the other three corners.

4 Valley fold the right corner into the middle.

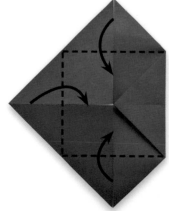

5 Do the same for the other corners.

6 Valley fold the top flap up.

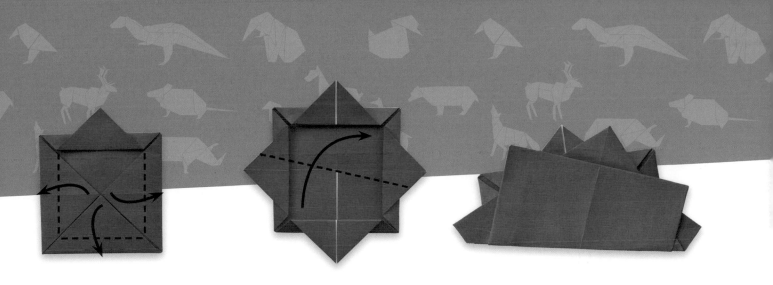

7 Do the same for the other flaps.

8 Valley fold the bottom section of the paper up at an angle, as shown, so that the triangles form an arc.

9 The paper should now look like this. This is the spiky back of the Stegosaurus.

PUT THE STEGOSAURUS TOGETHER

1 Slot the Stegosaurus's back into the body.

2 Stand the Stegosaurus up on its feet and you have one spiky origami dinosaur!

T. rex

Tyrannosaurus rex, or T. rex for short, was a fierce meat-eater with a big head and sharp teeth. Its name means "tyrant lizard king!"

START WITH A BIRD BASE

1 Find out how to make a bird base on page 8, and then place your paper like this. Valley fold the upper flap.

2 Take the right flap at the very back of the paper and swing it to the left, so that two points are revealed at the top, as shown in step 3.

3 Valley fold the bottom flap up to the top.

4 Valley fold the bottom corner of the upper right flap into the middle.

5 Do the same on the other side.

6 The paper should now look like this. Turn the paper over.

Pull

7 Gently pull out the tall point on the right into the position shown in step 8.

Pull

8 Do the same on the other side. Then mountain fold the tip of the central triangle.

9 Valley fold the bottom section over to the right as shown here.

10 The paper should now look like this.

11 Unfold, then valley fold the bottom section over to the left.

12 Unfold and you should have the crease marks as shown here.

13 Take hold of the left side of the bottom point and push it up and in to achieve the shape shown here.

Push

14 Flatten the paper to make a triangle at the bottom. Mountain fold the top section, so that the left side folds behind the right.

15 The paper should now look like this.

Triangle at top

16 Turn the paper so that the bottom triangle comes up to the top, as shown. Mountain fold the top point.

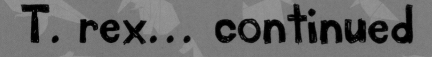

Push ►

17 Unfold, then make an outside reverse fold to create the head.

18 Tuck in the tip of the nose to make it blunt.

19 Valley fold where shown. Push down and back on the neck to bring the head down.

20 Mountain fold then valley fold the leg to make a step fold.

21 Unfold the valley fold. Make an inside reverse fold to create the foot. Do the same on the other side.

22
Push the head down a bit more to make it look big and scary. You have created the king of the dinosaurs!